Border Angels
THE POWER OF ONE

Border Angels
THE POWER OF ONE

by Enrique Morones
with Richard Griswold del Castillo

San Diego State University Press
San Diego, California | 2015

San Diego State University Press
Copyright © 2015 San Diego State University Press.

Border Angels: The Power of One is published by
San Diego State University Press, San Diego, CA 92182.

Nota bene: Border Angels: The Power of One is the second, corrected, re-titled, and
expanded edition of *The Power of One: The Story of the Border Angels* by Enrique
Morones, with Richard Griswold del Castillo, published by SDSU Press, 2012. A special
thank you to Bertha Hernandez, whose special editorial assistance contributed to the
evolution of this project.

Photographs in this volume are the property of the Border Angels and their
affiliated members and appear here with the permission of Enrique Morones.
Additional photography for this edition was provided by Pamela Calore,
Maria Teresa Fernandez, and the Border Angels website:
http://www.borderangels.org

Any mistakes of attribution should be mailed to SDSU Press, San Diego State University,
mc: 6020, San Diego, CA 92182-6020 for correction in future editions of this volume.

San Diego State University Press publications may be purchased at discount for
educational, business, or sales promotional use. For information write
SDSU Press Next Generation Publishing Initiative,
San Diego, California 92182 or email us at memo@sdsu.edu.

San Diego State University Press 5500 Campanile Drive
Arts and Letters 226, mail code 6020 San Diego, CA 92182-6020

ISBN-10: 1938537904
ISBN-13: 978-1-938537-90-5

Cover and book design by Guillermo Nericcio García and William Nericcio
for *memogr@phics designcasa* | http://bit.ly/memografix

PRINTED IN THE UNITED STATES OF AMERICA

"When it comes to immigration,
Enrique Morones is our moral authority."

Assemblyman Gil Cedillo
Author, California Dream Act

"My father, Cesar Chavez, led heroic grape workers around
Delano, California, in the longest continuing farmworker strike in
U.S. history in a profound statement of non-cooperation with a
farm labor system that exploits and impoverishes mostly immigrant
farm workers. Today, courageous members of Border Angels are
honoring the legacy of my father by making a powerful statement
against inhumanity and oppression endured
on our border by innocent immigrants."

Paul F. Chavez, President
Cesar Chavez Foundation

"Enrique Morones' story is remarkable and needs to be told.
He is a man of conscience who stands up to injustice by
simply being on the side of love and human dignity.
Let us all rejoice that an angel walks among us in this
fight for immigration reform, truth, and justice for all."

Josefina Lopez, playwright and activist
Author, *Real Women Have Curves*

"Enrique Morones is the finest example of the *Sí Se Puede*
attitude in service to those who risk their lives
in search of a better life."

Arturo Rodriguez, President
United Farm Workers of America

Dedication and Thank You

This book is dedicated to the greatest man I have ever met. My personal hero showed me and demonstrated all that is good in this world. Integrity. Faith. Family. Love. Patience. Hope. This book is dedicated to my father,Luis Morones, RIP, September 23, 1919—July 29, 2013. He's still my guiding light.

I also dedicate this book to the greatest human-rights activist the border has ever known and the spark that lit the flame of social justice for so many: Roberto Martinez (R.I.P.).

Last, this book is dedicated to the millions of migrants that cross borders all over the world in search of a better opportunity for themselves and their families. These people are the salt of the earth, and, thanks to them, we all have better lives.

I thank my beloved family and the thousands of volunteers who have joined and supported Border Angels and like-minded groups.

Special thanks to our board of directors: Ricardo, Sara, Octavio, Breezy, Dave, Dermot, Eduardo, Craig, & Greg

Special thanks to Pam Calore, our former outreach coordinator, artist, and photographer, and to Dulce Aguirre, our new, incoming outreach coordinator

A big *gracias* as well to Sophia, Raul, Mar, Micaela, Olga, Hugo, Estela, Joshua, Christauria, Keren, Mario, Oscar, Isabel, Jorge, Roberto, Daniel, Josefina, Max, Felipe, Sara, Benigno, Rita, Yolanda, Margarita, Remedios, Rosalie, Gil, Paul, Artie, Lidia, Heriberto, Elvira, Pamela, Laura, Roberto, Yoli, Hector, Gaba, and so many others.

Finally, a very special thanks to Ricardo Griswold del Castillo, for his patience and guidance in writing this book, and to William Nericcio, for his understanding and sacrifice in publishing it.

Ni Una Muerte Más, Reforma Ya!

Enrique Morones Careaga

Table of Contents

Introduction

Richard Griswold del Castillo
PROFESSOR EMERITUS, HISTORY AND CHICANA/O STUDIES
SAN DIEGO STATE UNIVERSITY

In the time it takes you to finish reading this book, another Mexican immigrant will die trying to cross the U. S.-Mexico border. This story is about one man's crusade to stop these deaths. For the past 25 years, Enrique Morones, the director of an organization called the Border Angels, has been fighting to bring an end to the deaths of thousands of immigrants who have been crossing our international border with Mexico. Standing a bit taller than 5 feet 10 inches and stocky in build, Enrique was born in San Diego of a strong Mexican family. He has dual Mexican and U.S. nationality—one of the first to receive dual citizenship—but he is also proud of being an American who loves this country. He wants the United States to be better, following the spiritual directions set out by his faith to love the poor and outcast.

Enrique is one of a number of human-rights spokespersons who emerged in reaction to the horrific number of deaths that occurred because of increased border enforcement policies under Operation Gatekeeper, which began in 1994.[1] Along with scores of activists on both sides of the border, Enrique has been an outspoken advocate for just and humane immigration reform as well as for an end to policies and rhetoric that are based on prejudice and ignorance that lead to suffering and death.

In this book, Enrique tells of how he came to dedicate his life to saving immigrant lives and became a spokesperson and champion for them when they have been attacked. Today his life has become a testimony to the power of love and compassion in confronting bigotry, fear, and hate. More than anything, Enrique wants to give a voice to the thousands of immigrants who are passed over and forgotten by the officials and media on both sides of the border. His mission is to give a human face to migrants and to offer them Christian compassion in food, water, and clothing.

---

[1]Operation Gatekeeper was a federal program of border enforcement that increased the staff of the Border Patrol, led to the construction of a new wall (in October, 1994), and increased the use of electronic technology, especially along the Tijuana-San Diego border. The area of application now includes Ciudad Juárez-El Paso and other border cities. One-third of the 2,000 mile U.S.-Mexico border has a wall.

Each year, thousands of undocumented immigrants cross the border into the United States and trek through the deserts and mountains of the Southwest trying to avoid the double and triple fencing and increased militarization of the U.S.-Mexico border. In the summer, hundreds die of heat exhaustion as the temperature soars to over 120 degrees Fahrenheit on the desert floor. In the winter, many perish from exposure as they try to cross the freezing mountains and deserts.

The Border Angels, which was founded by Enrique, is a group of volunteers who leave water in the deserts of the California borderlands in the summer and food and clothing in the mountains in the winter. Enrique, who is the main organizer, does not seek personal credit in saving lives, only that more people join him in getting Congress to pass immigration laws that will end these deaths by facilitating legal entry into the United States.

Enrique's story is fascinating and prosaic at the same time, filled with chance encounters and personal sacrifices. Told in his own words, it is a captivating tale of how he was influenced by his family (his parents and a grandfather, who was a major Mexican political figure of the 1920s and 30s, Luis N. Morones, founder of Mexico's first major labor union, the Confederación Regional Obrera Mexicana/Mexican Regional Confederation of Labor), his Catholic religious faith, national political figures like Ethel Kennedy (the widow of Robert Kennedy), and, most of all, by the immigrants' stories.

His full-time devotion to the Border Angels came at the end of his full-time job as vice president of Latino and international marketing for the San Diego Padres baseball organization. But his activism has focused more on organizing people than leaving water in the desert.

As a spokesperson for immigrants, Enrique has visited the canyons of northern San Diego, where immigrants live in caves and crude shelters. He led relief efforts for migrants during the 2007 San Diego firestorm. In February, 2006, he led cross-country caravans informing people about the plight of the migrants, asking the country to rise up and march against unjust actions, while demanding human immigration reform. He has appeared on television and radio programs like the "Today Show," Larry King, Bill O'Reilly, Don Francisco's "Sabado Gigante," and Lou Dobbs to argue against anti-immigrant prejudices. Each week he speaks before high school and college classes and in front of civic organizations to educate them about the tragedy taking place daily on our southern border. His involvement with the Obama administration led to him being consulted for impending immigration reform bills.

Enrique's mission has been to inspire other people to join the local, national, and international efforts to save immigrant lives and make the United States live up to its promise as a nation of justice and human worth. Enrique's story has no ending and is shared by scores of others who have dedicated themselves to the human rights of some of the most forgotten and oppressed individuals in our country. It is one testimony showing how the Latino people have responded to the sufferings of their compatriots. Hopefully, his story will inspire others to join community groups and other organizations like the Border Angels.

This book is a *testimonio* in the tradition of Latin American autobiography, a personal account that comments on political events of the day. In this kind of account, we gain an intimate perspective on public issues and get an understanding of them, bypassing a third-person narrative voice and a contrived objectivity. In this account, we get a feeling for the emotional and spiritual life of a human-rights activist. His account tells of his personal struggles to give a human face to the tragedies faced by Mexican and non-Mexican immigrants.

In his own words, Enrique believes in the power of one. By that, he means that even one person can make a difference by his or her actions. One person's caring can have big results, which is the moral of the Star Fish story told in Chapter 1. The key is to act according to the statement that has guided the Border Angels and Enrique's journey: "When I was hungry, did you give me to eat? When I was thirsty, did you give me to drink?" (Matthew 25:35).

The answer to this question is the challenge to us all.

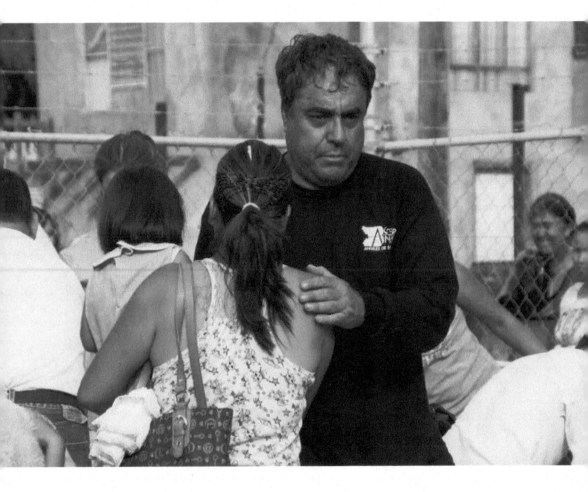

Another part of the Border Angels humanitarian work—here, Enrique Morones comforts victims of the Mexicali earthquake.

Chapter 1

Border Stories: The Power of One

One of the stories I have heard was shared with me by Juana Navarro, the mother of a young man who died crossing the border. What happens oftentimes, when someone dies crossing the border, is that we get a hold of his or her family to offer condolences and moral support. After I wrote her to give her my sympathy because her son had died in the desert, she wrote me back a very moving letter, which I still have. Here is a translation of part of the letter:

> Mr. Enrique Morones,
>
> . . . I still cannot accept the reality of the death of my beloved son, Marcelino Martín. What can I say about my son? That he was a noble, hard-working, honest young man who wanted to get ahead and to get to know a country so many young people dream about, in spite of my premonition as a mother. Even before he left, I knew something serious would happen to him . . . With tears in my eyes, I pleaded with him not to go north . . . His death has invaded me, and left me with so much anguish and pain in my heart and my soul; nothing has been able to lift it. . . . I don't know how he died, if in the desert or the river. However it was, it is irreversible and tragic. Since he left home, my anguish barely lets me sleep at night, and I haven't stopped crying. (See a full copy of Juana's letter in the Appendices.)

That's the story of thousands of people who have died trying to cross the border since the implementation of Operation Gatekeeper and stricter border security measures in the 1990s. No one knows for sure how many people have died crossing since 1994, but figures vary from six to ten thousand. None of the migrants anticipated that they were going to die. They all thought they would be able to get across and live the American Dream. They didn't realize their fate until it was too late.

I've talked to a lot of the families, and they don't realize how horrific the border crossing can be. The immigrants realize the danger too late, when they're out in the mountains or the middle of the desert or in the trunk of a car suffocating. In the letter I just quoted, the mother, Juana, grew more and more desperate because there was no word from her relatives in the United States, who were awaiting her son. The people in her village were giving her support when she got the message that he had been found dead. She didn't know if it was in the river or the desert. She still hasn't been able to recuperate.

That message in her letter, the wording of that message, is very powerful. I'll never forget that letter, because when I got it, it really moved me, and still breaks my heart when I think of it. I read that letter to President Felipe Calderón (Mexico's 2006-2012 president) as well as President Vicente Fox (Mexico's 2000-2006 president), and I've read it at many of the events we have had, rallies and services, such as those at the border wall. I've read it to people many, many times. When Maná (a popular Mexican rock band) came to San Diego, I gave a copy of the letter to one of the band members. About a year later, I was listening to a new record by Maná; they had a song called *"Pobre Juan,"* and I've always wondered how much influence that letter, if any, had on them composing that song, because there are some lyrics almost verbatim from the letter. Juana Navarro's message was very, very powerful. To this day, I have never received a more beautiful and, at the same time, sad letter.

Sometimes I hear the stories of the migrants who are alive, and sometimes I hear the stories of the loved ones of people who have passed away. When I talk about the deaths on the border, I think it is really important to personalize them. I know one of the things that motivated me to personalize the border stories was *Schindler's List* (the movie about the Holocaust). I remember when I saw that movie. Of course, like most people I thought how horrific that period in world history was; I think in terms of numbers—millions of people died during the Holocaust, about two thirds of them being Jewish. I think how horrible that is. But it's hard for me to capture what one million is, or even a thousand. I could picture maybe fifty or a hundred, but for me to imagine ten thousand or more people dying, it's hard to understand on a human level. But in Steven Spielberg's movie you see individual stories, and I thought that's very powerful to have these individual stories that personalize a mass tragedy.

One of the individual stories that I remember is that of Marco Antonio Villaseñor. Marco was a five-year-old boy who crossed the border for the number-one reason that migrants who are crossing from Latin America have today: economic opportunity. He crossed with his dad and some other men. They were heading for Houston where they had a job lined up. In his case, his mom didn't want him to go. His parents were having marital trouble, and the father brought the little boy anyway. They were going to have a smuggler take them to Houston in the back of a truck. There were about eighty people in that truck, and they soon ended up in Victoria, Texas. Marco Antonio became very thirsty and desperate so he asked his dad for some water, but his dad didn't answer. He asked the next man, and the next man. He asked the eighteen men around him for water, but none of the eighteen men were able to give this little boy what he needed. The reason was that his father and all the other men had already died; then Marco Antonio Villaseñor also died near Victoria, Texas, in May, 2003. When authorities and the driver finally opened up the semi truck, there were eighty people in the back of the truck, and nineteen of them, including the little boy, were dead. Of the eighty people about a dozen or so of them were women, and none of the women died. Given what the percentages were, some of the women should have died, but with their strength and maybe the help of the men . . . No one knows why, but it was very curious that only the men died. There's a book about this by Jorge Ramos, the Univision anchorman, entitled *Dying to Cross: The Worst Immigrant Tragedy in American History.*

When we organize cross-country caravans to dramatize the need for change (*Marchas Migrante*), it is very important to me to pay homage through stories like this, and so we do. We still hold vigils at places like Victoria, Texas. There, we met with some of the local community members, including a priest and family members of the victims, and we did a ceremony there at the gas station where the truck was found with the migrants. The truck had pulled over there, and the migrants were pounding on the sides to get attention; no one heard them. They were so desperate that they poked out the tail-light and wove a rag. Someone saw it and alerted the sheriffs. I think the driver fled, but they caught him. It remains the biggest mass killing of immigrants at one time in American history. The story of Marco Antonio Villaseñor is one I tell a lot, because, no matter how you feel about the issue, when you talk about a child it touches everybody's heart and personalizes the issue of thousands of deaths. People also die on the Mexican side of the border, as happened when 72 migrants died crossing from Central America to Mexico in Tamaulipas during September, 2010.

Before that tragedy was the story of Devil's Highway, where fourteen people were found dead in the Arizona desert. Their story is told by a local San Diegan, Luis Urrea, in a book called *The Devil's Highway.* Those are the kinds of deaths I am more familiar with, people dying in the desert. For me it is really important not only to get to know the families and the people around them, but to pay our respects and learn more about the the reason for their deaths. The larger cause is, the current immigration policy that makes it practically impossible for immigrants from Mexico and elsewhere to come here legally. Most migrants do not qualify for visas, so either they starve in their home countries or look for opportunities to survive, just like your ancestors. [2]

---

[2] In their policy statements, the United States Conference of Bishops shares the following pointed view: "there are insufficient visas to meet this demand (migration to the

The Starfish and Other Stories

The starfish story has been around for a long, long time. I heard it once from Mahatma Gandhi's grandson Ravi when he came to the University of San Diego. I was in the audience, and he told the story. I thought I finally had the source of the story, but afterward, when I went up and asked him, he said, "Oh no, my grandfather told that story as well." It is a very powerful one.

There's a man walking along the beach with his son, and as they are walking his son is picking up some starfish and throwing them back in the ocean. The father asks, "My son, what are you doing?" The son says, "Well, I'm picking up these starfish and throwing them back in the ocean." "But why?" says the father. "Because the tide has gone out, and the sun is so hot and they're dying," replies the son. The father says, "I can see that but there are thousands of starfish, and what you are doing doesn't make a difference." But the boy picks up the starfish and shows it to his dad and says, "Yes, it will make a difference to this one."

To me this story about the power of one is very significant because you never know, when you're doing something, who you are influencing. You never know who is listening to you when you are speaking. You might think that people are not affected by what you do or say, but some day someone might come back and tell you, "The starfish story and power of one really affected my life."

We all get frustrated. I know I do. But instead of saying, "What can I do about it?" I kind of say, "Well, the system should change," but we don't participate in making that change, so out of that story of the starfish—and I share it with the groups I speak with—I say the person who is going to make a difference is the person you look at in the mirror every day.

Most of the time you never come back in contact with the people you talk to. You might see them, but you don't know that it was you who inspired them. Maybe it was that one speech or lesson, or they saw you on the news. This reminds me of one of the more active people today, Micaela Saucedo, the executive director of Casa Refugio Elvira in Tijuana, a place that helps immigrant women. She was initially inspired by Bert Corona, a long-time immigrant rights activist. One day I

U.S. from Mexico). Close family members of U.S. citizens and lawful permanent residents face interminable separations, sometimes of twenty years or longer, due to backlogs of available visas. U.S. immigration laws and policies need to be updated to reflect these realities." See "Frequently Asked Questions about the Catholic Church's Position on Immigration," http://bit.ly/bishop_immigration (September 2010).

came out in the news talking about Gente Unida, which was a coalition we formed to oppose the Minutemen (a paramilitary anti-immigrant group), and all of sudden she called me. She introduced herself as Micaela and said, "I understand that you formed this coalition, and you have meetings." I said, "Yes we meet every week at Chicano Park."[3] She showed up at the next meeting. This was in 2005. She had already been active in her past and had retired, but now she became one of the most active people around, very supportive of Border Angels and Gente Unida.

Micaela and I first met Elvira Arellano when we did *Marcha Migrante I* back in 2006, at one of the stops in Chicago. Everywhere we go on these *marchas*, we don't know where we are going to stay or eat. We stay at people's houses. In Chicago, we met at a very famous landmark for the Mexican community, then went into a hall where I gave a speech about the importance of joining our call for marches. Then a young lady came in with *tamales* to feed us. That lady was Elvira Arellano. That was in February of 2006. Later that summer, she sought sanctuary in a local church, and she called to tell me of her plight. I thought, "Elvira Arellano?" I didn't know who she was. I just went along with her. Later, I Googled her and saw that she was on the front page of the Chicago paper. But I knew her as the *tamale* lady, not as Elvira Arellano, the lady who was to remain in sanctuary in a church for one year in Chicago because she didn't want to be deported and separated from her young son, Saul. She was deported a year later, however, and went through Tijuana. Through *Hermandad Mexicana* and Border Angels, a house was created called *Casa Refugio Elvira*, and Micaeala Saucedo, the woman who cold-called me in 2005, became the director. All this shows the connections between people and their stories, again the power of one.[4]

---

[3]Chicano Park is a community park located in Barrio Logan under the Coronado Bay Bridge in San Diego. It was taken over by the community in 1970 and today has the largest collection of murals of any park in the United States. For a history and pictures see http://www.chicanoparksandiego.com/.

[4]Since the first edition of this book appeared, several friends of the Border Angels have left this world—it brings me great sadness to share that Micaela Saucedo succumbed to cancer, September 1, 2013. RIP.

Migrant child in the canyon

Becoming an Activist

One of the more powerful events for me, one that changed my life, was in 1993. On April 23, 1993, my friend, Gil Hernandez, who was the community relations representative for the then Los Angeles Raiders, said to me, "I'm going to the funeral for Cesar Chavez. Want to go?" But I told him I couldn't because I had to give a speech somewhere. I wish I had gone with him, but I could not get away. Not long after, there was a big celebration of Cesar Chavez's life at East L.A. College. It was a big rally with a lot of people who had lobbied to change Brooklyn Avenue to Cesar Chavez Avenue and succeeded. They sat me with the Chavez family, with Federico, Paul, and Elena. They put me there because we had done a huge event called *"Reencuentro"* in L.A. where we also gathered signatures for the United Farm Workers. Our contribution to the campaign was quite small, but, in any event, they sat me there. Then this woman came and sat next to me, and we started talking. She asked me what I did. I said I was from San Diego and had been involved in the *Re-encuentro* in L.A. to bring communities together after the Rodney King riots.[5] But I said my biggest passion is the work that I started in 1986, going into the canyons in North County, San Diego, and bringing food and water to the migrants.

She wanted to know how it got started so I told her the story of how a friend of mine from the Elizabeth Seaton Catholic Church parish in Carlsbad, California, had told me about the migrants. My friend had said, "There are migrants living in the canyons and since you often collect things for Mexico's poor, how about here in San Diego?" Her name was Yolanda. I said, "What are you talking about? Where I grew up, in Golden Hill and at the neighborhood church where I went to grammar school, Our Lady of Angels, there are all kinds of migrants." My friend said, "Now where I live in Carlsbad, there are migrants that live in the canyons." I couldn't believe her. I couldn't grasp that concept so I started going up there. They had an outreach group from that church that would go into the canyons every Saturday, so I started going with them. I was really changed by that experience, and that's when Border Angels was born, although it didn't have a name yet. I started going into the canyons on a regular basis on Saturdays, once or twice a month, sometimes bringing friends and family members.

---

[5]In April, 1992, Los Angeles experienced the largest riot in U.S. history sparked by the acquittal verdict of the police who had beaten Rodney King, an African American. Fifty-three people were killed, and more than a billion dollars in property damage took place. The riot seriously divided the city along ethnic and racial lines.

I shared this story with the person who was sitting next to me at the Chavez memorial event. She was fascinated by what I told her. She wondered why I did it. I said, "Well, as a Catholic and because of my upbringing, I was taught to do the right thing. I was taught to avoid standing out." I wanted to avoid the media and stand at the back. I was a private person and just wanted to do the right thing. I didn't need recognition. She said, "No, people do need to know about it. Martin Luther King, Jr. said, 'Injustice here is injustice everywhere,' and my husband really believed that. He took a bullet for it, and his brother took a bullet for it. I recommend you get out there on the front lines and tell people about this." She said—and I'll never forget this— "You're going to have enemies, of course, but some of those enemies are going to be from your own community. They're going to get jealous or are not going to understand or be envious. But you have the passion, so I recommend that you get at the forefront of this issue."

This was 1993, and the climate was different: Proposition 187 (an anti-immigrant proposition in California), Pete Wilson (a conservative governor of California and former San Diego mayor), and the North American Free Trade Agreement (NAFTA).[6] As a result of this conversation, I said to myself, okay, I'm going to change my method of operation. The reason this woman influenced me so much was that, if there's a family that represents heroes in the United States, this woman's family is at the top of the list. It was Ethel Kennedy who spoke to me that day, the widow of Robert F. Kennedy, who had been assassinated in 1968.[7] As we were talking, lots of people came up to shake her hand and say hello, and maybe one out of the hundred who came by said hi to me. She jokingly said, "Well, a lot of people seem to know you." But it was just the opposite. She changed my method of operation.

---

[6] NAFTA was an international economic agreement. Proposition 187 was passed by California voters in 1994. It made it illegal for undocumented immigrants, especially the children, to use public services such as health care, education, and social services. After a firestorm of criticism by immigrant rights groups and international controversy it was declared unconstitutional by a federal court in 1999. The NAFTA by the U.S. and Mexican agricultural authorities lowered tariffs and resulted in the ruin of many Mexican small farmers, who consequently became undocumented immigrants. Subcomandante Marcos was the mysterious leader of the Zapatista movement in Chiapas, Mexico. Since 1994 he has led the mostly indigenous people in a war against the Mexican government and its support of NAFTA.

[7] Robert F. Kennedy (RFK) was the brother of slain president John F. Kennedy. Robert was the Attorney General of the United States 1960-1964 and then was elected Senator from New York. He ran for president in 1968 and was assassinated shortly after he won the California primary.

I also remember in San Diego meeting in Barrio Logan at the Santa Fe Restaurant with Roberto Martinez, who I regard as the greatest immigrant rights leader on the U.S.-Mexico border. He was talking about the actions they were going to take on Proposition 187, and he would say we need people to do this and that. I would say, "OK, OK, you need someone. I'll be there." After my conversation with Mrs. Kennedy, I went from being a good soldier in the back to wanting to lead.

We all have defining moments in our lives. It could be some sort of a tragedy. It could be good fortune, or coming across somebody who deeply affects us. It depends on how you respond. There are times in my life when I wished I had responded a different way. But in this case, my life changed. Being introduced to the migrants in the canyons and meeting with Ethel Kennedy were the two key events that influenced my life.

Enrique Morones, first person to receive dual citizenship with Mexico; on Enrique's right, Nobel Prize winner, Dr. Mario Molina; to his left, Mexican President Ernesto Zedillo.

Chapter 2

Growing Up on the Border

Roberto Martinez was a well-known human rights activist whom I admired and considered my best friend. Tragically he died on May 20, 2009, after a long fight against diabetes. Roberto was one of my heroes and mentors, a man who inspired many people by his quiet, persistent dedication. Like me, he was born and raised in San Diego, and his early life experiences shaped his later activism. He told the story of his early life in a chapter in the book *Chicano San Diego*.[8] I want to retell it here to show how events early in life can shape people's activism.

> I was a student attending San Diego High School in the early 1950s. Frequently the police would stop me as I was coming home from school, and sometimes they would put me in jail and then turn me over to the Border Patrol for deportation. This happened about two or three times a month. The fact that I was a fifth-generation U.S. citizen didn't seem to matter. My family had lived in the relative tranquility of a farm community in East County, but in 1945 we moved to downtown San Diego after my father was discharged from the service. It was an enormous cultural shock for me. However, nothing could have prepared me for the terror and psychological trauma of being arrested or threatened with deportation by police and the Border Patrol. Looking back, I realize now how *Mexicanos* in Los Angeles must have felt during the massive roundups by both police and Border Patrol in the previous decades.
>
> . . . After I graduated from high school I got married, and in 1965 my family was one of the first Chicano families to move to Santee into a community called Carleton Hills. The day before we moved in, I went to check on the house to see if it was ready. To my surprise, workers were removing the wall paneling from the living room and throwing it in the front yard. When I asked them why, they said that the house had been vandalized the night before. When I looked at the panels, the words "get out of town, wetbacks" were carved into the panels. There were also swastikas scattered throughout the paneling. Although I had experienced racism before, this was the first display of overt racism directed at me, and my family. This would be my introduction to the kind of racism and violence I

---

[8]Richard Griswold del Castillo, ed., *Chicano San Diego: Cultural Space and the Struggle for Justice* (Tucson: University of Arizona Press, 2007), pp. 223-26.

would encounter in my work at both the border and in the north and east county with farmworkers.

A month after we moved in, a cross was burned in front of the home of a prominent black doctor and his family that had also just moved in. They also sprayed swastikas on their walls and broke their windows. Within a week they moved out.

By the early 1970s several more Mexican families had moved into Santee. Some of the children, including mine, had begun attending Santana High School.[9] Also at this time the Youth Klan Corp was actively recruiting members at Santana High School. The school administrators allowed this recruiting to occur on campus year round. No one had ever challenged them on this racist policy. By 1973, I began emerging as a leader in the community, primarily as a leader in the *Mexicano* community. We, along with other *Mexicanos*, felt isolated socially, culturally, and politically, in east San Diego County. A few years later, I began receiving complaints that the white kids at Santana High were attacking the Mexican kids after school. Following one particularly vicious attack on the Mexican kids by white youths, including Youth Klan Corps kids who wore T-shirts that read, "white Power" on one side, and Youth Klan Corps on the other, I received a visit that would change my life forever.

In June of 1979, three Mexican women called me at home and asked if they could bring their three teenage children who had been attacked at Santana High School the day before. That very afternoon the three women brought their three children, two boys and one girl, to my home. The two boys were badly beaten about the face. The girl had bruises on her face and neck where she had been choked by a sheriff deputy. The three claimed that a group of white boys, including members of the Youth Klan Corps, were waiting after school with boards and bats for the Mexican kids. As usual, the Mexican kids were outnumbered. Shortly after the melee began sheriff deputies arrived to break up the fight. However, instead of arresting the white boys who had initiated the fight, the deputies not only arrested just the Mexican kids, but badly beat them in the process. As the kids were relating their horrifying experience to me, all of my own experiences with police and the Border Patrol came rushing forward, and I could feel the anger building up inside of me. I knew then that I could not remain silent.

---

[9]Santana High School is located in Santee, a community in San Diego County, 15 miles east of downtown San Diego. The high school received national attention in 2001 when a student there shot and killed two students and wounded thirteen others.

Roberto did not remain silent. The rest of his life he spoke out and acted to defend the rights of Mexican immigrants. Along the way, he became an internationally recognized activist.

My path toward becoming involved in the struggle for human rights for immigrants was different from Roberto's, but it came from the same sources as his: a love of family, a strong religious faith, and a sense of moral justice.

Like Roberto, I was born and raised in San Diego. My family lived in a working-class neighborhood near Barrio Logan. We always spoke Spanish at home, as we do to this day. This is a tradition that I am passing on to my family. I speak Spanish to my brothers and sisters as well. But as soon as we went out into the yard or out in front of the house, all the neighbors were American kids, and we'd speak English. I grew up with both languages. We still speak Spanish with our parents, and outside it was all English because the neighborhood was all Anglo. Now you have more of a mixture. That's why I'm a firm believer in bilingual education and knowing at least two languages.

I grew up in this Catholic, very traditional Mexican family. All five of us—Luis, Laura, myself, Nora, and Pedro—as a result of our parents' upbringing are bilingual and bicultural. We're very proud of our Mexican roots. We are also proud of and grateful for the United States, the country where we reside and have made our lives. I have dual nationality and am proud of both countries. All of us have been heavily influenced by my parents, who have been married for sixty-five years.

We were a working-class family. My dad had two jobs. He's a very humble guy, not one who looks for any kind of attention. He's my hero without a doubt, a model of what a man should be, always providing for his family. My mom didn't work, although later in life she did work a couple of times. She wanted to work. All the kids were out of the house. She worked in a clothing store and loved it. My dad worked at first in Mexico's Fish and Game Department here in San Diego (the reason the family moved here), then returned to the airline business and directed Aeromexico's operations in San Diego for 20 years. He also worked at a little market down the street so we could have extra income. My little brother Luis also worked there. When I grew up there was lots of love in the family among the kids. There still is.

Upon graduating from Saint Augustine High School[10] in 1974, I got a four-year scholarship to the University of San Diego (a Catholic uni-

---

[10]Filmmaker Greg Nava also graduated from St. Augustine High some years before. His film "El Norte" influenced my life as to the realities of the migrant struggle.

versity). My parents couldn't afford it, but I got the scholarship. I didn't know what I was going to study. I remember in my freshman year I took courses like psychology, oceanography, French, and karate because I was interested in those subjects. In my sophomore year I started getting interested in marketing. There was a really good business professor there, who said, "San Diego State University is one of the top ten business schools in the country so you should consider it." The University of San Diego didn't have an international marketing program, but San Diego State did. I ended up transferring to San Diego State with the intention of running track and and graduated with a degree in international marketing. Then I went back to University of San Diego to go to graduate school and get my Master's degree long after I had graduated. I ended up going for a Master's in executive leadership begun by friend Ken Blanchard at the University of San Diego.[11]

All this played into my life—the religious schools, the academic training, going to church. But my faith and family values were the key. Long-distance running was important, too. It created a discipline and stamina that I would draw on later. When I used to run back in the 70s (120 miles a week) it was not like it is now. Now you see people running and think nothing of it. When I used to go to Mexico and run, people thought I was a maniac. "What's that guy doing running in the middle of the day?" Now you see people running in Mexico and all over the world. My status as a maniac is still unclear.

There are life lessons to be learned in running a race. I remember one of the first Special Olympics. There was a 100-yard race. The gun goes off and all the Special Olympics kids run as hard as they can. Then one by one they stop as they hear someone crying, they turn and see one of the runners, fallen. They all go back and help the runner up. They all hold hands and walk across the finish line together! The crowd goes wild, gives them a thunderous, standing ovation. The power of one!

I did not have the kind of racial confrontations that Roberto Martinez had growing up, but I did have a strong sense that people deserve to be treated fairly, with compassion. This came from my religious faith, which Roberto also shared. Before he became a full-time activist with the American Friends Service Committee, Roberto had a full-time job working in the business world, and he worked with the Catholic Church as a part-time organizer. In later years he served on the Board

---

[11] Ken Blanchard is the author, with Spencer Johnson, of *One Minute Manager* (New York: Berkley Books, 1983). The popular book has sold over 13 million copies and has been translated into 37 languages.

of the Border Angels. After I graduated from college, I also had to learn to balance a full-time job with part-time activisim, and eventually, as with Roberto, it was the activism that became a full-time job.

The wall—Operation Gatekeeper—on the Mexican side of Friendship Park. The art featured here is by Permin Brieu, commissioned by the Border Angels.

Chapter 3

Becoming a Full-Time Activist

I believe that activists are made, not born. It usually takes a series of events, almost accidents, to lead up to a person becoming involved in human rights actions. It is a gradual process. Mar Cardenas is a very interesting story. Mar's name is Marta, but she goes by "Mar." Mar is a person who is now well known, but when she joined the Border Angels human rights movement she was not. She had never been an activist.

Every year we hold what are called *Marcha Migrantes*. These are caravans of people who travel across the country meeting with local communities to support them in their struggles and let them know about our work in advocating for immigration reform. On *Marcha Migrante III* in 2008 Mar joined us after she heard about it from a friend. I remember we went to our first stop in Holtville in the Imperial Valley at the cemetery where more than 700 unidentified migrants are burried. She called me and said that she had missed us at the start and wanted to join us now but could only stay a day. I told her that it was kind of hard to find us now because we were on the road to Los Angeles but that she could meet us there. She said, "Fine." The next day we met up in the Placita Olvera in L.A. about noon. She arrived and heard the speeches and was very excited. The *Marcha Migrante III* participants spent the night at Plaza Mexico in our sleeping bags. Mar had only expected to be with us that day. She told me, "I'd like to go a little further in the *Marcha*." I told her, "You can go as far as you want." She had to get some clothes so she called her husband Gary in Santee (an eastern suburb of San Diego where Roberto used to live), and he drove up with some clothes. I thought she would be with us a few more days. She was very shy.

In the *Marchas Migrantes* there is always a core group of a dozen people or so. At every stop, I like them to tell their experiences to the people we are visiting. Sometimes it's just a sentence, and sometimes people like to go a little longer. At first Mar would say just a few words like, "Hi, I'm Mar Cardenas. I'm excited to be here." But toward the end of the *Marcha*, she would beg to talk, and she would be the one—besides me—to talk the most. I was really impressed by that. Her background was that she was a bilingual education teacher. She knows Esperanto. She knows Spanish. She's a really nice woman. She joined us, very enthused, and went with us all the way. Every *Marcha* we have had a person who suddenly gets moved by the experience and joins us for the entire *Marcha* (Pablo, Carmen, Josefine, Keith, Mar, Lupe, among others).

When Mar came back from the first *Marcha*, she became more and more involved with Border Angels. She became our official listserv person. Then she started getting involved with the Unitarian Universalist Church, and she started inviting me to many of her events. Now she is a lay minister with the church. When the Mexicali earthquake took place in 2010, we put a call out to the public to collect food and clothing. We used her church in Chula Vista for the drop-off place. Again, Mar became very involved. We made seven or eight trips to Mexicali with emergency deliveries of five tons of supplies directly to the victims of the Easter Sunday quake. A lot of the local media got to know her through that. I would ask her to talk to the media, and she got more and more exposure.

On the last major action, we participated in the march in Phoenix in 2009 against Arizona law SB 1070 (criminalizing undocumented immigrants under state law), and the very first person arrested in this protest in all of Arizona was Mar Cardenas. They took a picture of her in her yellow shirt saying, "Standing on the Side of Love" from the Unitarian Universalist Church. I was having a support action in San Diego when I found out. She was in jail for two days in Phoenix and told me later that when Sheriff Arpaio[12] came through, she reached out and told him, "I love you." Arpaio just ignored her. Mar went from that shy person who just wanted to be with us for a brief time to being the first activist arrested in this protest against the Arizona law. Now Mar is very active and very involved with Border Angels as well as a lot of different groups. She learned the ways to be effective as a spokesperson working for immigrant rights.

My own introduction to activism came while I was working. My professional career has taken many twists and turns, but every step of the way I have learned valuable lessons that have prepared me for my Border Angels work. I have worked in retail, radio, tourism, marketing, and even major league baseball. All these experiences led up to my full-time involvement with the struggle for justice for immigrants.

In retail, working at Bill Gamble's clothing store in San Diego, I learned how to deal and interact with people in all sorts of situations. It was there that I learned to value teamwork and the importance of setting and reaching goals. In tourism, while at Krystal Hotels of Mexico, I met Yolanda, who told me of the migrants in the canyons. (This is the story I would later tell to Ethel Kennedy at the Cesar Chavez rally.)

---

[12]Sheriff Joe Arpaio is a controversial sheriff of Maricopa County under investigation by the federal government for his aggressive methods in the treatment of Mexican immigrants.

We all have moments when we have to make a choice, to accept things as they are and pretend you do not see what is going on (as most people do), or make a change when you see what is unjust and try to make it better. That is what I chose, to make a positive difference.

I went into the canyons Yolanda had mentioned and was mortified and very sad to see men, women, and children living in the open air in the dirt. How could it be possible that the wealthiest country in the history of the world allowed the very people who picked our food, took care of our children, and built our homes to live in canyons without shelter, running water, or electricity? How do you communicate with your families back home? Are you getting medical attention? Do your children go to school? I asked and was overcome by the sweetness, kindness, and sincerity of these hard-working people, the salt of the earth, the best of us, our indigenous brothers and sisters. It was right then and there that the Border Angels was born, in the canyons of Carlsbad in 1986. We did not have a name yet, but a movement was beginning. I knew I had to do something.

I was soon to have one of those key moments we all face in life. I was introduced to our brethren in the canyons, and I began my regular visits to them, first alone, then with others to see the truth of Martin Luther King's statement, "Injustice here is injustice everywhere."

In 1990 I got a job working as the director of Stouffer Presidente Hotels in Los Angeles. That's when I moved from San Diego to Los Angeles. At that time there was a lot happening in Los Angeles. There were the freeway shootings. I remember I would go visit my girlfriend Sandra in the San Fernando Valley and then come home at night. The California Highway Patrol would stop me and other persons of color as suspects. One such person was pulled over and nearly beaten to death. His name was Rodney King. What was unusual was it was caught on video. A video of that event led to riots. I was in Mexico and saw the riots on the TV, and at first I thought it was in another part of the world. I couldn't believe it. Los Angeles was under martial law. My return flight came in at night, and I used to live right by the airport, maybe ten minutes away. It was kind of eerie because when I got in I took a shuttle, and there was nobody on the street. It was a tense situation.

A friend of mine, Armando Charles, thought of the idea to have an event at the Convention Center, called the "*Reencuentro*," to rediscover your roots. The idea was to bring the communities together, the Latino community, the Korean community, the African American community, the white community and others because of all the tension in the city. Armando was the point man for this event, with myself and friend Magda Rojas. It was a huge success. We had ten thousand people there. We were going to have Cantinflas (Mario Moreno), the very famous Mexican movie star, as the *padrino* of the event, but he passed away right before the conference, so the person who ended up being the godfather of the event was Ricardo Montalban. We had him, a book festival, business people, tourism, activism, and the petition to change the name of Brooklyn Avenue to Cesar Chavez Boulevard. Cesar had just died. (Today the Eddie Olmos Book Festival carries on this tradition.)

A few weeks later they had a rally at East L.A. College to support the street name change. I went and sat with the Chavez family and had the "power of one" moment I previously mentioned. Meeting Mrs. Kennedy was was very influential in my life because her husband had faced lots of opposition that had ultimately cost him his life.[13] I will never forget her words when I told her about my visits to the canyons and the migrants: "People need to know about it because they want to help. Just remember. You're going to get attacked by people who don't agree with you but also by people within your own community."

The San Diego Padres Experience

I came back to San Diego in 1994, a watershed year in immigration. In California they were trying to pass a terrible, racist bill, Proposition 187. The United States, Mexico, and Canada passed the North American Free Trade Agreement (NAFTA), which allowed commerce to cross borders but not people. The result of this agreement was increased poverty for small farmers in Mexico, who couldn't compete with U.S. agribusiness, and an increased migration north. In Chiapas, one of the areas most severely affected by NAFTA, Subcomandante Marcos led an indigenous uprising against the government. Also that year was Operation Gatekeeper and increased militarization of the border—a wall was built between Tijuana and San Diego. After Operation Gatekeeper, the number of migrant deaths increased dramatically so that one or two would die every day!

I wanted to continue my activism but had to earn a living, too, so I wrote many of the baseball teams about the need for diversity and how they should really be reaching out to Latinos. I wrote letters to some football teams, too. But the only team that responded was the San Diego Padres, which was because the San Diego Padres had two brand-new owners whom I saw on television, Larry Lucchino and John Moores. They bought the team in December of 1994. In their press conference they said, "We're going to have a winning team. We're going to

---

[13]See footnote 7.

make going to games a fun family experience." I thought, "They always say that." One thing they said caught my attention. It was, "We're going to have a winning team off the field." I knew that they meant that the new team president was going to be successful in the community. Larry Lucchino was very community oriented. I sent my letter, and pretty soon I got a phone call. Larry Lucchino's secretary said, "He would like to meet with you." I went in a week later, and we began dialoguing on a regular basis. I thought this is the head guy here. I was very impressed. I said, "You don't know me." He said, "I do know you. I see you in the news. I like what you're doing. We should carry this a step further, but through baseball." He was referring to my activism. I had become more visible and gotten involved with issues like Proposition 187, Operation Gatekeeper, and NAFTA. I was sometimes in the news speaking about these issues.

I began working with the Padres at the end of the 1995 baseball season, without a doubt the greatest period in my life, spanning 1995-2001. I met the love of my life, Stephanie, but unfortunately we didn't marry. I was a huge sports fan and had gone to every Padres opening game since their first year in 1969, and now I was working for them. I'm sure I knew more about the team and its history than almost anyone who worked for the Padres. I also learned a lot from Larry Lucchino, the team president and my boss. There was resistance from some of the people there because they had really never done anything to reach out to Latino fans. I told Larry I would join the organization under three conditions. One, we had to start the first-ever department of Latino marketing in a major-league sport—and be completely devoted to that. He called it Hispanic, I called it Latino, but he was the boss. Two, I would be the one to run that department and give it all its direction and report directly to him. I didn't want to have roadblocks. Three, my activism came first. Sure, baseball was important, but I wasn't going to stop my activism because of my job. He gave me the green light. The rest is history. We had the first-ever regular season games played in Mexico—*la primera serie*—on August 16-18, 1996, in Monterrey, Nuevo León, Padres vs. the New York Mets. We had the Domingo Padres Tecate program, where people would bus across the border to the Sunday game and we opened a Padres store in Tijuana. Our program was a huge success. We went from 50,000 Latino fans prior to my working with the Padres to 800,000 Latino fans when I left at the end of the 2001 season!

My experiences with the Padres helped me with the Border Angels organization. For example, when we had planned to have buses transport fans across the border, I had my first meeting with Doris Meissner, who was the Commissioner of the Immigration and Naturalization Service. Of course the people on the Domingos Padres Tecate bus program had papers, but we said this could be a model for making it easier to cross the border. It was very exciting. However, at the end of the 2001 season, Moores and Lucchino went their separate ways. Moores told me, "Thank you very much. You taught us how to do it. We don't need you anymore." It was his decision, but I think that he was influenced by a couple of people in the office who didn't agree with my Mexican-outreach emphasis or my activism. San Diego Latino community leaders like David Valladolid and Ray Uzeta called me, saying, "Look, we can do a major campaign to get you back in. It was outrageous what they did. You know, a boycott or something." Although I appreciated their support, I said that wouldn't be right. It wasn't right what the Padres had done, but something told me that if I were to get my job back it would be really tense. It might be good for me personally with the money and all but not for the community, and the community came first.

While with the Padres, I also became the first person to receive dual U.S.-Mexican nationality. I went to the Mexican national palace and got it from the hands of then Mexican President Ernesto Zedillo. It is a wonderful memory. For the ceremony, ten people were selected from around the world to receive the documents directly from the president. I was the only one born in the United States, as the others had been born in Mexico. I was the first to apply, so when I was called up, the media went wild with photos. For the others, apart from Nobel winners like Dr. Mario Molina, there was little attention. I did not understand the attention. Was it my work with the Border Angels? Was it being the first to apply? Was it being a member of the San Diego Padres? No. Actually, it was the fact that I had brought a signed baseball to give the president. It said, "From the first citizen (me) to the First Citizen (as Mexican presidents are called)." When I looked down at my new document, number 0000000001, the President playfully tossed the ball in the air and caught it. That caught the media attention and made the front page of Mexico's national papers in June of 1998.

The highlight of it all was that my dad was there. The media were interested in this story; *The National Review*, which is a very conservative magazine, interviewed me. The interviewer asked all these questions about loyalty and divided loyalties. I said, "If more people had the spirit of a dual nationality this would be a better world." He asked, "What if there was a war?" I said, "If you're proud of wherever you are from, that's good. The U.S. is where I have made my life and I am very proud to be Mexican. This country has been very kind to my parents and my family. Many other countries have dual nationality. Other countries like Canada and France have dual nationality with the U.S. Did you interview people who have these?" He said, "No." I told him that a lot of his questions had to do with the race issue, that if more people had dual nationality it would help solve conflicts.

There are serious issues between the United States and Mexico, but we should be working together in building bridges of communication and not fences of separation. We should be embracing people with dual nationality, people who have dual cultures. There are really very few people in the world who are 100 percent indigenous to their native land. Almost everyone is of multinational origin. The blood I identify with is the indigenous, although I also have Spanish and Italian blood. But I don't identify with that European bloodline. I identify proudly as Mexican. If I'm asked about my loyalty, it is to this planet. Loyalty doesn't mean that you are against others. It means that you are proud of who you are. Working for the Padres confirmed this basic value.

Angeles de la frontera, **Border Angels, and Don Francisco**

Thanks to my "leaving" the Padres, I was able to spend a whole year doing missionary work, formalizing the Border Angels. A year later, I accepted an offer from a local radio station to host my own talk show, "*Morones por la tarde.*" I invited Roberto Martinez join me as a co-host. He expressed some interest, but we soon realized that he couldn't do it. He was a very quiet guy, and that's not a strength when you have a talk-radio show. But Roberto was my first guest. My second guest was another good friend, Carlos Hernandez, who was the catcher for the Padres during the 1998 World Series.

In 2003, I continued to work as a talk-show host. Jaime Bonilla, the station owner, was sure I would be good at it. He said, "You're going to fall in love with it," and that's exactly what happened. I had been interviewed before, but it is a lot different to be an interviewer. I'll never forget the first show, in January of 2003, from 3 to 5 o'clock. I thought, that'll be easy. The host who was already there, Marco Antonio Blásquez—he's still there—was to show me the ropes. He had had me on his show a couple of days earlier and promised to help me when I started on Monday. Monday rolls around, and my first two guests were Roberto Martinez for the first hour and Carlos Hernandez for the second. I told my dad, "Why don't you show up toward the end, just to check it out. It might be exciting for you to see it, and I'll ask you a couple of questions." All of a sudden it's five minutes to three, and there's nobody there except René Mora, the radio operator. The show starts, and there are two or three minutes of commercials. Then it's "*Morones por la tarde,*" and I'm all by myself. We're live so I have to talk. I say, "Oh, hello everybody. I'm Enrique Morones. I'm really excited to be here," and I'm looking at my watch, thinking, where's Roberto? I said, "Let me tell you a little something about myself." I thought that would take ten or fifteen minutes but it took only two or three minutes. Here, I had told my entire life story, and I'm thinking it's probably 3:15 now. I look at the clock. It says 3:05, so I say, "Well, I have this project called Border Angels" and start talking about the group; it's now 3:10. I had absolutely nothing else to say. Finally, Roberto comes walking in. Immediately, I want him to go on, but he wants to calm down. I go, "no, no, no." "Now Roberto Martinez..." We talk for five minutes and then go on break. He tells me he had been held up by traffic. He was with me the rest of the hour. I learned right then to make sure the guest always arrives early and to have a backup plan.

I had some well-known guests, including Dolores Huerta; Peter Camejo; Congressman Dennis Kucinich; Jeffrey Davidow, U.S. Ambassador to Mexico; Carlos Moreno, one of the California Supreme Court justices; and playwright Luis Valdez. Most of my interviews, however, were everyday community leaders and members. It was important to let the community know what was happening and how they could get involved, informed, assisted, or assist. We were a huge hit and won several awards.

The most unusual interview was with a guy named Bryan Barton. He was a Minuteman. When the Minutemen started in April of 2005 in Arizona, he caught an undocumented immigrant and put a tee shirt on him. It said, "I went to the U.S. and all I got was this tee shirt." He thought that was really funny. I said, "What you did was terrible. He came to the U.S. looking for work, and you made a joke about it." Barton was eventually fined for what he had done. He is the same guy who would paint the steps at Chicano Park—which are red, white, and green—red, white, and blue.[14]

Barton was also the same man who opposed our big march, on April 9, 2006, protesting Congress's proposed law against immigrants. As one of the main organizers of the march in San Diego, I was in front of some 100,000 people with a megaphone shouting, "*El pueblo unido jamás será vencido.*" Two undercover cops came up to me and said, "The Minutemen have their counter demonstration on the other side of the County administration building, all 30 of them. Enrique, we need to pull you aside. There's a neo-Nazi guy up ahead." I looked up and I saw him. I saw that it was Barton, a young kid maybe two years out of college, age 22 or 24. Seeing him, I said, "Why should I have to

---

[14]Chicano Park is a community park in Barrio Logan, San Diego. It has the largest collection of Chicano murals in one place in the United States and is a meeting ground for community celebrations and protests.

step aside? Pull him aside. You guys should drag him out of there," and they did, for his own safety.

When on the show, Barton and I spoke about the Arizona incident. He was crying. He had been e-mailing me, saying he was not a racist. But I told him, "You are, by your actions." Although he had some of his friends call in, we had dozens of other callers who really put him in his place.

There was one other guest, a super-right-wing Latino guy, who phoned in a couple of times. Finally, I had to say no more because he was saying the same thing over and over and not making any sense. This guy came up to me when I was at a public event with my family. He was sitting in front of me, turned around, and asked, "Are you Enrique Morones?" I said, "Yeah." "I'm so and so, and I'd like to talk to you about what you said today on the radio." I said, "Listen, I'm relaxing with my family. This is not the time. I'm not interested in speaking. Go back to where you're sitting." Just imagine if he had been an unstable, violent person with a gun. I realized that talk-show people are highly vulnerable. I learned that when you speak out, you expose yourself.

I learned a lot. The show lasted for three years, from 2003 to 2006. I had to stop because of security issues and threats. July of 2005 was really busy. I had to spend the nights out at Campo (a high desert community about 80 miles east of San Diego on the border). I had guest hosts, which was the beginning of the end. Bonilla said, "You can't have a show and have all guest hosts." I told him the same thing I had told Lucchino: "My activism comes first. I'm sorry." I stopped the show but came back to the station ocassionally.

Backlashes

Working in radio prepared me to establish the Border Angels as an organization that could work more effectively in the face of anti-Mexican immigrant prejudice. As a result of my outspoken support of immigrant rights, I started to get lots of hate mail. Strange things began to happen. One of the scariest incidents took place in my building. One day as I was at my mail box getting my mail, my neighbor commented, "You had a lot of excitement at your place yesterday. The police, the firemen, security people were at your unit." I said, "Well, I didn't hear anything." Apparently, someone had jumped the fence and entered the unit just above mine. The tenants were a couple and their two children. This was at three in the morning. The wife went out on the balcony screaming, "Help, help, help!" This was at three in the morning. My neighbor, who lives across the way, didn't hear anything, either. But a guy who lived across the little garden area, who is a pilot, came over and helped the husband hold this guy down until the police came. It wasn't very clear if this was a random act or not. There had been some suspicious things taking place, like calls. I am, like anyone else who might be involved in this, extra cautious.

One time, a man was calling at all hours and leaving hate messages. Finally, a police lieutenant told me he was going to call the harrasser. He did, and it stopped for a while. Later, I saw this same man for the first time at Friendship Park when we returned from a *Marcha Migrante*. He was one of the young men screaming stuff and threatening people. Very rarely do I feel threatened. I do record scary phone calls, however, and give them to the police. They say things like, "We're going to get you," and, "We know where you live." The San Diego Police Department and law enforcement do a great job sharing intelligence and offering protection, a real help in dealing with the threats that activists always face.

The one man who has a police blotter is Jim Chase, founder of the San Diego Minutemen. Once, we were at a television studio in northern San Diego for a cable show's series of interviews. The guest before me was Dan Muñoz, Jr., the editor of *La Prensa*, a well-known Latino weekly in San Diego. We were in the green room while Raul Contreras, a conservative talk-show host and anti-Minutemen, was being interviewed. Dan and I were laughing and kidding about the interview, and Dan says, "Well, the guy they're interviewing after you is going to be really interesting." I asked, "Who is it?" He said, "Jim Chase." Chase and I had had many run-ins at the border. Dan goes in for his interview, and I'm sitting there alone with the producer. Well, Chase comes in with his wife, looks in and sees me. He tells the producer, "Do you know who that is!" He starts screaming, "That's Enrique Morones! I want to kill you! How dare you have him in here!" The producer tried to calm things down and said, "Mr. Chase, you have to control yourself." He was extremely agitated, and I remember thinking some day he would do something irrational. I didn't know if he had a gun on him. I remember I had my recorder, so I turned it on and remained calm. There was a lot of commotion. Finally he stormed out. The producer told me that we needed to file a police report about this. I told her to please do me the favor of monitoring my car while I was being interviewed. I didn't want this guy committing vandalism. Nothing happened, but I did file a report. I even had a meeting with San Diego's District Attorney, Bonnie Dumanis, and, incredibly, she said, "Well, he said he wants to kill you. Not that he's going to kill you." Now I realize the difference, but this was not a random event. He's got a gun, and his friends have guns. Roberto Martinez was with me during this meeting, and he was really mad at Bonnie. Many members of the community are disappointed with the D.A.'s office. Her response to hate incidents has been horrible.

The radio experience was useful in preparing me to establish the Border Angels as an organization that could work more effectively despite all the anti-Mexican immigrant prejudice generated by a few individuals. I learned more about the media and to deal with difficult individuals. I learned to argue calmly and confront racism and bigotry in a public forum. I learned that people are really receptive to hearing the truth.

Sheriff Joe Arpaio debating Enrique Morones.

Chapter 4

The Birth of the Border Angels

Organizations and their leaders cannot be as effective if working alone. Often, alliances are the most effective way to bring about action. This was shown to me when we worked with Dolores Huerta,[15] former Vice President of the U.F.W., during *Marcha Migrante I*. We left San Diego on February 2, 2006, and our first major city stop was Los Angeles. In every place we try to get a point person to coordinate our arrival with local events. In Los Angeles, the point person was Dolores Huerta. She was very excited and met us at the Placita Olvera about six o'clock in the evening. There were Aztec dancers and lots of celebration. A *Virgen de Guadalupe* image was placed next to the Placita Church. It was very exciting to have Dolores Huerta as our host. She is a tremendous person who has done a lot for the poor and oppressed in our country. She gave us a very inspirational message, and we talked to everyone about the importance of rising up against HR 4437.[16] I told the crowd about what was really going on along the United States-Mexican border. Dolores has always been concerned about the need to protect the immigrant children. A few months later she said, "We have to say to our immigrant community who are not citizens, they can help us because they pay taxes. They have a role in the political process. They have a right and a responsibility. When Cesar and I were in the C.S.O., we worked to end the Bracero Program, and then we worked to legalize over a half a million *braceros*. Cesar and myself and the people in the C.S.O. and the Farmworkers Union, we had to put a new face on the issue of immigration. One of the faces that we have to emphasize is that of the citizen children. We have to go back to our communities to emphasize that we have to give them sanctuary."[17]

---

[15]Dolores Huerta worked with Cesar Chavez beginning in the 1950s and became a major leader of the U.F.W. for the next thirty years—Huerta is co-founder of the U.F.W.
[16]The House of Representatives passed HR 4467 on December 16, 2005. It proposed making it a federal crime to be in the U.S. without documents and imposed penalties on those who assisted them while in the U.S. Widely criticized as criminalizing undocumented immigrants and those who helped them, the bill never passed the Senate. A nationwide series of protests and marches, the largest outpouring of support for migrants in U.S. history, helped stop HR 4437.
[17]Sept. 9, 2006, speech, National Latino Congreso
http://www.youtube.com/watch?v=WtKkUUuV-8o

Marcha Migrante I, with Dolores Huerta.

Her commitment meant a lot to us. When we met with her in Los Angeles, she told us that she really liked the idea of holding a march in Los Angeles to bring together those who opposed HR 4437. We had been advocating that idea, too, and other people picked up on it. She wanted to have the protest on March 26th because every year on that date we have the U.F.W. march to commemorate the Delano-Sacramento Pilgrimage.[18] The local activists who formed a coalition wanted to have their protest march on March 25th, a day earlier. Eventually, almost one million people participated in the March 25th event; the U.F.W. had its march the next day. The Border Angels, the U.F.W., and the March 25th Coalition all had worked to make this event happen.

Lessons learned by the U.F.W. helped in my thinking about the purpose of the Border Angels, which came into existence in 1986, but did not have a name until 2001. Prior, my work on the border had been very informal. We weren't the Border Angels until Don Francisco (host of a popular Univision program) gave us that name while I was a guest on his show, "Sabado Gigante." I liked the name for the group. I worked full-time getting the 5013C status, setting it up in a more structured manner. Now we're at a whole different level. Back then, we were in a growth period, with maybe 50 volunteers, most of them students or visitors just passing through town. We wanted to get more serious. The border deaths continued to accumulate, so I began to dedicate myself to developing and formalizing the Border Angels.

To me, Roberto Martinez is definitely a Border Angel. I knew of him in the 1980s, but I met and started getting to have regular meetings with him in 1990-1993, during the Proposition 187 campaign. At the beginning, I was still living in L.A. I would come to San Diego on a regular basis to go to the canyons in North County. I would meet him and three or four other people at the Santa Fe restaurant in Barrio Logan to talk about Proposition 187. I remember that he was undoubtedly the leader, but he was the quietist. He was the leader who commanded the most respect. He had the most experience and knowledge. I might ask, "How are we going to have an event on Saturday and this other group is going to have one on Sunday?" He would say, "Well, this other group doesn't like to work with this group." I saw that his style was non-conflictive. He quietly went about his work.

---

[18]On March 26, 1966, a group of farmworkers and their supporters led by Cesar Chavez and Dolores Huerta walked from Delano, California, to Sacramento to dramatize the need for labor reforms for farmworkers and the sufferings of the poor. It was timed to arrive in Sacramento on Easter Sunday.

However, Roberto wasn't always quiet. He told me about when he went undercover to help a migrant. A *Union Tribune* reporter—I'm not sure who—went with Roberto. They went to this Escondido bar where the local law enforcement were harassing our migrant brethren. They went in and had a beer. Sure enough, about 11 o'clock some Escondido police came in. A couple of Mixteco people were playing pool, and the police went up to them and started harassing and belittling them. Then, one of the Mixteco guys went to the bathroom, and the police followed. Roberto went in, too. The police started pushing this indigenous man, and Roberto challenged them. "What are you doing?" he said. "None of your business. Get back out there." "It is my business. I work with human rights." What happened was that they started going after Roberto, and they took it outside. That's when the reporter from the *Union Tribune* identified himself, and they backed off. The cops were really mad.

Roberto had a lot of stories. Another one was about how in National City he challenged the ongoing corruption in the police department. He started taking pictures of some officers who were harassing migrants in a parking lot. The police saw him and did not like it. They surrounded him and were going to arrest him, but the shop owners and community members began to surround the police. It was a true "Mexican standoff," and eventually the police left and let Roberto go.

Roberto always had a calming manner. He was always quietly paying attention. Then, he would have some really powerful words of wisdom. For example, I'd ask him, "Roberto, why didn't you speak out when this guy said this at the meeting?" He'd tell me that he had a history with certain people and all the ramifications that would come out of his confronting him. He knew how to deal with people, the most challenging thing for any of us.

I would go to his office at the American Friends Service Committee, bringing him cases. He would give me advice. Every once in a while he would join us, or we would join him, for events and press conferences and that sort of thing. Most of that time I was just the guy standing at the back. The vocal stuff gradually built up after I moved back to San Diego from L.A. I really got to know him during the Proposition 187 campaign, and we became friends. When he retired from the American Friends Service Committee we became even closer. He wanted me to apply for his position, but I didn't really actively pursue the A.F.S.C. director's job. Roberto is sorely missed there, as he truly represented the Quaker spirit of the American Friends.

After Roberto retired from the A.F.S.C., I asked him if he would join us, the Border Angels. There was a time when we were having a couple of sponsors, and so every month we would give him a small donation just to help him out. We did that for a couple of years. Roberto took care of the books and helped us with grants. He continued with the Border Angels until his final days. He was my right-hand person and best friend. Among all those who are actively out there in human-rights work, Roberto was in a class of his own.

Migrants and Minutemen

I continued going to the deserts and canyons. I had heard about a chapel that the migrants had built in the canyons. I wanted to find out where it was so I got a hold of someone who knew, and I started going there about 2003. They had these park benches, this image of the Virgin of Guadalupe in tile, and a little table for the priest. There are a couple of documentaries made by John Carlos Frey, who filmed in the canyons. There was a man who took care of the chapel, named Generoso, perfect for his name, Spanish for generous, because he is a very loving person. He speaks Mixteco but very little Spanish. He's from Oaxaca. The reason we eventually had to take the chapel down was the Minutemen's terrorizing migrants in the canyons. There was a Spanish-language reporter from Telemundo in L.A. named Maria Luisa Garcia, who came down to the canyons to film. I didn't think anything of it. Then, two weeks later, a report comes out on N.B.C. about the migrants of the canyon, saying that they were rapists and thieves. I was horrified. I was in Maryland giving a talk when it came out, and someone called me so I called the police chief and the pastor, Father Frank, who handles the church that ministers to the migrants. "Father Frank," I said, "This is unbelievable. This is insane. This is crazy." Local hate-radio jock Rick Roberts started saying, "Let's camp with the illegals," making fun of it, so I talked to Police Chief Lansdown and Father Frank. I said, "This Saturday, as you all know, they are planning to go into the canyons and camp out with the migrants. These are Minutemen and other extremists. We can't allow that." The guy in charge of the canyon area was a policeman named Boyd Long, a really nice guy. He told me, "Enrique, we can't have those counterprotesters (the people from our side). Are you planning a big counterprotest?" I told him, "Tomorrow we can get 5,000 people to counterprotest." The Minutemen were calling people from all over, which meant they could have fifty people there. But I didn't want this confrontation to take place because the ultimate losers would be the migrants in the canyons. The Minutemen just come back and harass the migrants when we're not around. I told the police, "Look, I can tell people not to counterprotest, but I am sure that some people will show up anyway. You've got to assure me that you won't allow those guys, the Minutemen, to go into the canyons." We didn't have a protest. The Minutemen had about 50 people, and about ten from our side showed up. Some of them were local residents who didn't want the Minutemen there. That day, in 2009, the Minutemen did not go into the canyons. But a few weeks later they raided the canyons and destroyed the migrants' housing.

A couple of months after that the police raided the house of the three people who they suspected were involved. Fortunately, they didn't discover where the chapel was, but we knew they would find it eventually and decided to take it down on the *Día de Guadalupe*, December twelfth. It was raining so we couldn't do the mass. It continued raining, and we weren't able to take it down until the day of the Epiphany, January sixth. There's a great picture I have of us walking out with Generoso holding the image of our lady of Guadalupe, and Cristauria L, the lady who leads the chapel.[19]

Eventually, we started having a rotating place to hold services. We didn't have any chairs or anything, but a priest would come. Finally, after a couple of months, a really nice gentleman said, "You can do it on my land." He's from Taiwan, which is really neat because he's a Buddhist. He's not a Christian, but he is more Christian than most Christians because of the way he lives. At the peak, there were about 3,000 people living in those canyons: Poway, Peñasquitos, Carlsbad. Now I would say there are a fraction of that. We have taped a few as part of a public-service announcement. These guys in the canyons are the same guys crossing the deserts. Today, as numbers in the canyons have dwindled, you don't have women and children like you did before; mostly, it is men.

The Migrant Trail

One human-rights activity that has strengthened me and many others is the Migrant Trail experience. The migrant trail is held annually by *Derechos Humanos* in Arizona, headed by Isabel Garcia and Kat Rodriguez.[20] The idea of it is to go on probably now the most traveled trail for migrants coming to the U.S. from Mexico. It used to be through Baja California, but since 9/11 it's been through Arizona. They meet in a place called Sasabe, Sonora. Altar is a tiny community that had very little commerce and now it's primary business is related to migration. All the stores there sell backpacks and water jugs and baseball caps, all the things you would need for the trail. They go from Altar all the way to

---

[19] See below, p. 91.

[20] *Derechos Humanos* is a human-rights coalition based in Tuscon, Arizona. It is dedicated to stopping the deaths on the border by raising awareness of the need for meaningful immigration reform. Their activism in protesting discriminatory laws and racist actions is highlighted by their annual Migrant Trail walk.

Sasabe in vans. A 12-person van might have 40 people in it. They get dropped off in Sasabe, and that's where they start walking.

What *Derechos Humanos* did was to initiate The Migrant Trail, where they start in Sasabe. We meet in Tucson at a church and then we get rides to Sasabe, Sonora, to a church. We have a brief meeting there with a mass, and the priest tells us a few stories about migrants who go through there all the time, and they are very religious. Their first stop is the church in Sasabe, Sonora. It's right on the border. When I participated in 2008, there were about 60 people from many sponsoring organizations. Border Angels was one of them. The first day we meet some of the people there, a few of the families, the people who live there. We ask them what it's like living in the community. Then we start walking. We walk from Sasabe to the border, less than an hour's walk. We cross at the regular checkpoint, and, as soon as we cross, we give our documents to somebody in our group who puts them in a lock box. That way, when we are crossing we have no documents, the powerful symbolism of solidarity with our migrant brethren. We keep on walking. The first day it's only about six or seven miles. This is during the last week of May. Every day you walk and then camp out. You have your backpacks. You do have trucks with you to carry sleeping bags, tents. They provide the food. We always camp out about noon because then it's too hot to continue. It's dead time from noon to five in the morning. We post guards at night. We have talks, and it's just wonderful.

The next day you walk about 12 miles. You start walking about six in the morning, and you don't stop except for regular rest stops every three to five miles. Along the way we are carrying these crosses that bear the names of real people who have died. In 2009, I drove to Tucson and told everybody that I wasn't going to be able to make the walk. Roberto Martinez had just passed away. I had a cross made for Roberto, and a young lady named Cruz carried it. Margo, a lawyer with the group, said that on Wednesday, the one-week anniversary, she was going to talk about Roberto.

We do this for about six days. The final day we arrive at a park in Tucson. It's a very spiritual experience. Of the sixty people who walked in 2008, a few had to get medical attention or be hospitalized because it's very difficult, and you walk at a very fast pace. I used to be a distance runner, and I know about pacing. I told the woman who led the group, "You're going too fast. The sun is going to get to us." We needed to start an hour earlier. The most important person in the march is the last person because that person is struggling to catch up. It's very challenging but nothing compared to the migrant's real march. When I went, in 2009, there were about 40 people. It's a wonderful experience. They charge fifty dollars to do it. When we crossed, we ran into migrants. Two guys came into the camp one night, and they said that their wives or girlfriends were having a hard time so we sent someone out to help. We told them they could join us if they wanted. But they wanted to stay on their own. *Derechos Humanos* does great work.

Firestorm

The San Diego firestorm began on Sunday, October 21, 2007. I was at the migrant chapel in the canyons attending a regular mass. You couldn't see anything unusual that day, but the next day you could see ashes in downtown San Diego so I shot up to where the migrants were working in the fields. I was really worried because there were no fire services in the canyons. We didn't know how bad it was until Monday. It was a horrendous event, the largest evacuation of a city since the U.S. Civil War. I was horrified to see these guys working there in the fields. I have a friend who is a doctor and also a teacher at U.C.S.D. medical school, Dr. Eduardo P. Tanori. He goes into the canyons with some of the students so they can become more socially conscious. He does blood tests and exams among the migrants. I called him and said, "Dr. Tanori, we need you. Can you join us? I can give you the location, and you can go see these guys in the fields." He came out there with me.

We did a call-out for help for victims of the firestorm on Monday. Greg Morales, a member of M.A.P.A (the Mexican American Political Association), a friend of mine, called me and said he was really worried and that we should do something. He and I got together at Chicano Park. At first we sent e-mails, and little by little got some response. I also called K.P.B.S. and Univision television. Within an hour people showed up from K.P.B.S., and they put out an alert, along with Univision. By now the fire was really escalating. We ended up getting 500 carloads of supplies at Chicano Park from Monday, October twenty-second, through Saturday, the twenty-seventh. I contacted Tommie Camarillo, head of the Chicano Park Steering Committee, and asked if we could use the park. She, as always, was very supportive. People would pull into the parking lot and drop off items and then pull out. We had a constant flow. Border Angel people like Micaela Saucedo would be the ones who would run the supplies out to the areas that needed them. Micaela went to East County; some went to the Rincon Indian reservation, others to Potrero. I would go to the canyons.

We ended up getting lots of volunteers. One of them was a paramedic. I asked him, "Can you come with me?" He and I, along with Dr. Tanori, went into the canyons and began looking for the inhabitants. I told the migrants that it was too dangerous to stay. One of migrants told me something I would have never thought of, just to show you the purity of their hearts. When I was saying they needed to get out and how the winds could shift, the guy asked, "Who's going to shuttle out the squirrels and animals who live here?" I thought there is such a beauty in that, to think about the animals. They didn't want to go. But there were a few who were real sick. I made some phone calls to house these people. A dozen or so were transported to a house near Balboa Park. They stayed with us for about four days.

The day that we were heading back, I was outside, early in the morning, getting ready to go. I couldn't find them. I said, "Where are they? They're so responsible." I was looking all over. Somebody asked, "Are there five of them?" I said, "Yeah." "Well, they're sitting in your back seat." They were so small I couldn't see them. They are men but small. They were just sitting there quietly waiting. One of them was an older man who needed help. Through the Mexican consulate we were able to get an airline ticket for a woman and her baby so they could go back to Mexico. The others stayed with us in the little house near Balboa Park.

We ended up setting up drop-off locations throughout the county: in South Bay with Diane at the Environmental Health Coalition and our friends from the Unitarian Universalist Church; in East County with Estela at the Center for Social Advocacy; and in North County with the churches. I'll never forget the firestorm response because it was multicultural. We advertised it as a call to help the underserved community, which is mostly people of color. The people who responded were from all ethnicities. Somebody who came down—and I didn't know she knew who I was, but I knew her—was Bree Walker, who was on TV and who, at that time, was on Air America. She knew about Border Angels. She came down with her son, a fourteen-year-old. The media were very responsive. Adolfo Gonzales, the police chief of National City, came down. Fr. William Headley, the priest in charge of the U.S.D. Peace and Justice Center, came down in street clothes, and I took him in my car to see some of the work we were doing. You had people from all walks of life come and volunteer. Some of the neediest people were down there doing most of the work. Martin Eder and Susan Friedman from Activist San Diego and Tanya Winter contacted a group in New Orleans called Common Ground.[21] Malik, one of the co-founders of Common Ground, and Sharon came to San Diego. During Katrina they had done something similar to what we had done, especially for the underserved African Americans in New Orleans. The rea-

---

[21]Common Ground is a non-profit group that seeks to provide quality low-income housing and combat homelessness. They also work with families facing housing crises.

son they came out was so we could meet. We took them with us to the canyons and the Indian reservations and had a big press conference where Malik talked about New Orleans, and I talked about the similarities with San Diego.

There is a good news story on our website by Thelma Gutierrez from C.N.N. One thing that happened was that prior to the fire they were not very interested in the migrants in the canyons. When the fire happened they all became very interested. We had people from the big media, like *The New York Times*. I remember telling them, "We're standing here being passed by doctors and lawyers in their BMWs taking their stuff because there was mandatory evacuation of the North County, and across the street in the fields the migrants were still working. There was no mandatory evacuation for them, no reverse 911 calls to their cell phones in Spanish." We went and talked to the supervisors in the fields, and they said, "It's up to them. They can go if they want." I said, "They crossed three or four borders to get here and there is a line of people waiting to do their job. They're not going to stop. You've got to close the fields." But they wouldn't. I was furious. I flew to Mexico City that week and met with President Calderón and alerted him to this travesty and soon went toe to toe with Governor Schwarzenegger.

I was called downtown to do an interview with N.P.R. and friend Brooke Binkowski. Suddenly the Terminator (Governor Schwarzenegger) showed up for a press conference. I had media credentials then because of my radio show. I went inside, and I was right in the front row. He came in and looked at me, probably thinking, "Where do I know this guy from?" He started his press conference, and he said how San Diego did a great job with the fire. I got really mad and told him, "Which San Diego are you talking about? It's not the one that I've been in. Yesterday you were at a Chargers game, and, while you were there, there were migrants out there with no aid from the city." He had Chief Kollender (San Diego Sheriff) and Jerry Sanders (San Diego Mayor) right next to him. He looked at them, hoping for them to back him up. But they knew me and avoided eye contact. I got really brave so I said, "Don't be looking at them for help. They know that there was nobody out there." There was the Terminator, furious but trying to keep his cool. We were going at it. I said, "They won't leave because law enforcement is working with the Border Patrol. They shouldn't have to worry about their immigration status right now, and the ones who are in their apartments are scared to leave them because you have checkpoints set up to check their IDs, and they don't have IDs because you won't pass the drivers license bill." He started screaming, "And I'll never pass the driver's license bill." That ended the press conference. As we were walking out, Kollender pulled me aside and said, " You know, you have a point. We shouldn't be checking people's documents right now." I said, "Well, you've got to stop it because people are afraid and if they die inside their apartments, you're going to be responsible for scaring them." We sent out notices to the Border Patrol about this, and the head of the Red Cross joined me on it. We told them that when they went to Qualcomm Stadium, the largest official evacuation site, not to go in Border Patrol uniforms to check for papers. They did, and I was furious. They ultimately changed their policies. Our case was mentioned before Congress.

Politics

I have had the opportunity to meet many presidents starting with Jimmy Carter. I was involved in the Al Gore campaign. I even met the latest President Bush. But my most serious involvement in politics was with the Obama campaign. It was set up so that people could be directly involved to help him. Usually, when someone runs for office, whether mayor or city council, he or she gets people to walk door to door for him or her along with other similar strategies. But I had never, ever encountered such a sophisticated organization enabling anyone to get involved. I liked Obama early on and, like most of the country, had no idea who he really was. I remember when Hillary Clinton came to San Diego and we met. I had also met Bill Clinton, who I liked.

My involvement with helping organize human-rights activities as well as working a little bit in the political arena made me realize that the Border Angels needed to expand its message to a larger area in order to bring about real change. This was the motivation behind the organization of the *Marcha Migrantes*, a series of cross-country s to connect with grassroots organizations and to educate people about the migrant deaths and get them to take to the streets. Three million did in 2006. That is what I now call the Immigrant Spring of 2006.

Migrants on the Mexican side of
"the wall" across from "El Norte."

Chapter 5

Marcha Migrante

On December 30, 2005, Guillermo Martínez Rodríguez was killed on the Tijuana-San Diego border. He was a young man from Mexico who lived in Tijuana. He and his brother, Agustín, decided to cross over into the United States. They climbed over the wall in Colonia Libertad. In Colonia Libertad they had decided to build a second wall. It's an area where now there is barbed wire. Agustín and his brother hopped over the first wall. Guillermo was on top of the second wall when a Border Patrol officer saw them. Guillermo saw that the Border Patrol was there and that he was going to get caught so he jumped off the wall and started running back. He was in between two walls, set to jump over the wall into Tijuana. Augustín was running, too, when he heard a gunshot. He jumped over the wall and started yelling to his brother, Guillermo. But Guillermo didn't respond. Agustín saw Guillermo lying in a pool of blood, between the two walls, bleeding to death. Agustín jumped over again and dragged his brother back to the wall. He carried him over the wall and took him to the hospital. Guillermo died the next day, on December 31, 2005. That story and many more like it are what motivated the Border Angels to begin the *Marcha Migrante*.

The *Marcha Migrante* is really a caravan of volunteers who travel across the country to meet with other community groups to organize rallies, marches, prayer vigils, and cultural programs raising awareness of the need to end the deaths in the desert and to implement immigration reform. We have had now seven *Marchas*, and they all have been extremely important.

When I go to speak to students in schools, they all want to know how they can get involved. They are all fascinated by the *Marcha Migrante* idea. I tell them that *Marcha Migrante* was born in the spring of 2005, during a watershed year. The Minutemen started in April of 2005, and HR 4437 was passed by a Republican-controlled Congress (a resolution making it illegal to help undocumented immigrants). It was similar to 1993-94 with the border wall, NAFTA, and 187; in 2005 you had anti-immigrant sentiment escalating like never before. You had people like Lou Dobbs going from being a financial commentator on "Moneyline" to hosting Broken Borders on CNN, slamming Mexico, and making very racist comments. The Minutemen were also becoming more active. In April, 2005, when the Minutemen started in Arizona, I contacted Arizona's premier border activist, Isabel Garcia, of Tucson-based *Derechos Humanos* and asked if she would like our help. She said, "Yes," and I said, "We don't want to have any physical contact; we have to adhere to nonviolence." That's when I decided to form a group called *Gente Unida*, united people, a coalition of groups along with the Border Angels. Through peer pressure of other organizations we ended up having more than 60 organizations join, and together we were successful in maintaining nonviolent action. Because of the success we had in shutting down the Minutemen in California, we developed an even bigger following.

In December, 2005, the House passed HR 4437, the James Sensenbrenner bill. When that bill passed, which was like 187 on steroids, I thought, "This is unbelievable. We've got to do something about it." Basically, HR 4437 made it a federal crime to help undocumented people and promoted spying on your neighbor, criminalizing the undocumented worker. HR 4437 would prohibit giving them food, shelter, spiritual consolation, and the like. It was pending to be voted on in the Senate. Many of us wanted to organize people to let Congress know how we felt.

In addition to the horrible implications of 4437, people didn't know about the deaths on the border. They really didn't know what the Minutemen were all about, and we needed to bring attention to this issue. In November, 2005, I was having lunch with some activist friends in Riverside County. I told them I had this idea from a few months back and that I couldn't keep it to myself anymore. I wanted to go across the country and go to Washington, D.C., drive across and see if people wanted to join in national marches and make a lot of noise about the issue of HR 4437 and other injustices affecting immigrants. People responded favorably. This was the origin of the *Marcha Migrante*.

As I said, the spark that began the *Marcha Migrante* and the formalization of the marches was the shooting of Guillermo Rodriguez in December, 2005—this was the final straw. So we decided to hold a prayer vigil. It came out on the front page of *La Opinión*, and at that prayer vigil I announced the *Marcha Migrante*. I said, "We're doing it. We're going across the country, and we're going to Washington, D.C. Does anyone want to join me?" I just threw the question out there.

I remember we had a meeting over in Salazar's Restaurant on Market Street in downtown San Diego. Roberto Martinez, Fr. Fabrini from Our Lady of Guadalupe, and two or three other people were there, and I said we are going to do this thing called *Marcha Migrante*. "I think that by going across the country from community to community we can get people to march in the streets." I thought it would be very powerful if we visited communities and asked them what they wanted to do. They asked, "When are you going to do it?" and I said, "February 1. It's going to take the whole month, till February 28." Then Roberto said, "You know, February 2 is the anniversary of the Treaty of Guadalupe Hidalgo," and Fr. Fabrini said, "And it's also the *Día de la Cande-*

laria, the Feast of the Presentation of Jesus at the Temple." I said, "Well, February 2 it is. It has both religious and historical significance so that's good enough for me." I had a press conference and announced, "We are going to have a *Marcha Migrante* and go across the country. Does anyone want to join us?" I had no idea if anyone would. I had an old beat-up car, and I decided we're going to leave.

On February 2, 2006, we left, and I think we had about 25 cars. The first stop was one that we have had every year, the Holtville Cemetery, where we share the stories of the migrants who have died. People usually say, "I had no idea." There, they can visually see 700 bricks that are the grave markers that say John Doe or Jane Doe, and it's very moving. There are people buried under those bricks. When we left, the story I shared with the group was from the Book of Luke from the Bible. It tells of Jesus, who wanted to go around telling people about justice, peace, and love. When he said he was going to go and a couple of people said they were going to join him, he said, "Oh, come with me. Come as you are," and they said, "No. We have to go back and tell our families that we are leaving and get our issues in order." He said, "Come as you are. If we go to a village and we are not received, we will dust off our sandals and go to the next village." I'll never forget that when we left on February 2, 2006, some people came as they were. They weren't planning on joining us. They were just planning on going to the rally. In all the *Marcha Migrantes*, there's always someone that gets so moved that he or she joins us for the entire journey.

We ended up having 111 cars in total join us along the way. The most we had on a given day was about 30 cars. From San Diego to Washington, D.C., and back, 40 cities in 27 days in 20 different states we went and saw people across the country, telling them what was taking place on the border and the border deaths. We needed to put an end to HR 4437. We couldn't let the Senate vote on it and not have the background information. We needed to let them know about Guillermo Martínez Rodríguez. We needed to let people know about the realities of the Minutemen. We needed to ask the people to rise up and march!

In the first *Marcha*, there was a lady named Mercedes from El Salvador, who met us in Los Angeles. In El Paso, another lady, named Carmen, just hopped in one of the cars. Then there was Josefina in Dallas. In the second *Marcha* there was Kevin. I remember that after a few days I said, "This guy's been with us. Who is this guy?" He was wearing the same clothes all the time, and he was with us most of the time. In the third *Marcha*, it was Mar Cárdenas. As I said, she went from a shy person to being the first person arrested in the anti-SB 1070 protests in Phoenix in 2009. The story of Josefina Villarreal is a classic. With Josefina we were doing *Marcha Migrante I*, which was very successful.

When we went to Los Angeles, Dolores Huerta met us, and other people were there who were later involved in the March 25 march (when more than 800,000 people demonstrated their opposition to HR 4437) listening to me talk. We spent the night with people who later ended up being the key organizers of the March 25 march. Then we went to Fresno and stayed at various people's homes. I stayed at the home of an undocumented person who had one of the most unbelievable stories of crossing the border that I have ever heard. He insisted that I stay at his house. Very humble, I remember that he said, "Don't park your car in the driveway. Park it there, right next to the window." You could hear gunshots in the background. I and two or three other people stayed with him and his wife. Of all the places we stayed, including some very nice homes, this hospitality has never been outdone.

We went across the country and did this in a variety of places. Sometimes we did a prayer vigil, sometimes a rally, or we would talk to students of the area. In Dallas, we did a rally right in front of the book depository building where President Kennedy was killed. Some of the better-known people who came from Dallas were the president of L.U.L.A.C. (Mexican American civil rights organization), Hector Flores; Juan Hernandez, who used to be in (Mexican) President Fox's cabinet; and a lot of community people. We usually have two or three people speak at these events, and I would always be the main speaker. I told the story from Luke, come as you are. I was done, and a woman was crying. She comes up to me and says, "I was so moved by your speech. Can I join *Marcha Migrante*?" and I say, "Oh, absolutely, come as you are." She says, "No, I can't come as I am. I have to go back. I live in Fort Worth. But I'll join you later. I'll catch up with you later." I thought, well, I'll never see her again, but I said, "Great, fantastic." The woman's name I would find out later was Josefina.

We traveled at a pretty fast pace, 10,000 miles in 27 days, with two or three stops per day. We'd go seven, eight, sometimes nine hundred miles a day. I wanted to make a point of crossing in Louisiana because of what had happened with Katrina. We crossed in the north near Shreveport and spent a night there. I think it was there where all of a sudden I got a call from Josefina, who asked, "Where are you guys at?" She was very passionate. Here was a Latina by herself in an old car. She joined up with us, and I thought, "This is pretty powerful." I asked her, "What motivated you?" and she replied, "I was really inspired by the speakers, but one of the stories you told was that you said along the way you had seen several signs." I said, "That's right. I have seen several signs." She said, "I want to see some of those signs." I said, "Well, I have nothing to do with those signs. They come from another place. It's not me. I believe it's God." She said, "Well, I believe in God, too." I said, "That's great, but I don't want you to come along and then be disappointed because you didn't see signs." The very next day after that conversation, we were driving along, and I was thinking about what Josefina had said. As I was thinking about that I looked up in the sky. It was a beautiful clear sky with not a cloud in it. All of a sudden I looked over to the left, and there were three clouds, long clouds. Apparently, three jets had come by earlier, and their vapor trails had intersected with the clouds making three perfect crosses, like at Calvary. The one in the middle was the highest. I was thinking, "Holy Cow! This is unbelievable." I called everyone and told them we were going to slow down for a bit. I called Josefina and told her, "Remember that sign you wanted to see? Take a look in the sky over on the left." I saw her car shaking. She was crying, and so was I. Unbelievable. There were other signs that happened on other marches, but this moment was one that I'll never forget.

The spirit of the *Marcha Migrante* was to go across the country and to work with the local communities, to let them decide what date they wanted to take action, and then go to Washington, D.C. We went there, met with members of Congress, and held a prayer vigil. We met with the Kennedy staff and a bunch of other people. Then we headed back and did the same thing on the way back. We returned on February 28. Cardinal Mahoney in L.A. came out with a statement saying that the Catholic Church was opposed to HR 4437. On March 2, I went to Los Angeles to have a press conference to announce the marches and the anti-4437 March of the twenty-fifth. On March 10, we had the march in Chicago, which had about 400,000 people. On March twenty-fifth, we had about 800,000 people. On April ninth, we had about 100,000 people here in San Diego. I know it wasn't just because of *Marcha Migrante*. Nobody knows exactly what it was. It was a series of things, some of which had happened before I was born. The *Marcha Migrante* was the turning point. It doesn't matter to me who started it. What matters to me was that it happened and that it worked, the biggest marches in the history of the United States. That's why we called it *Marcha*. We were originally calling on people to march.

An example of how the *Marcha* can affect national policy came when we had the *Marcha* in 2006. It was the best example of how the Border Angels could educate as well as work toward effective change in the immigration laws by making contact with the grassroots organizations as well as policy-makers across the nation.

Border Angels at work in the high desert

Chapter 6

National Politics and the Border Angels

Activists have to do more than give speeches. They have to advocate for and help the poor where they find them. For example, during one of the *Marcha Migrantes* we were traveling from Tucson to El Paso. It was a long drive, and we were getting tired, so we stopped part way in Demming, New Mexico. We went to this motel, one of these 30-dollars-a-night places. We were loaded down with stuff. We had some money from our fundraiser in Tucson and some food that people had donated.

I went in to negotiate with the guy for six or seven rooms with four people in each room. When I went in I saw something in the bushes. I went over, and, sure enough, there were some people in the bushes, eight people, seven men and one woman. They were migrants from Querétaro, Mexico. I spoke to them and told them who we were. I told them we had some water and food if they needed it. I looked and saw that they had gathered their jewelry together. I asked them, "What's going on?" and they said they had been abandoned by the smuggler and were on their way to find some work. I asked, "Why are you gathering all your jewelry?" They said, "we need to raise a little bit more money to get a room." I said, "How many rooms are you going to get?" They said, "Two rooms." I said, "Well, that's a lot of money you have there, more than you need." They said, "Well, the rooms cost $250 a night." I said, "Where did you get that information?" They replied, "That's what the guy told us at the front desk."

I told them to just wait there. I went inside the motel office, and I read the riot act to the clerk. He told me that the owner had told him that's what he had to do. I asked for the owner, and he came out. I could tell that he was a little bit concerned, and I decided to exaggerate a little bit who we were and what we could do. I told him that we worked very closely with Human Rights Watch. I told him that these people needed a room, and they were going to pay exactly the same rate as us. I told him, "If you call anybody like the immigration authorities, we're going to shut your place down." That's where I was exaggerating. I told him that the migrants were going to stay two nights and that when we came back we would be in touch with these people and if there was any trouble we would know. He was really scared by now, so we paid for the two rooms and went and got the migrants.

The next day, before we left, we gathered some food and money for them. I knocked on the door to give both to them and to say good-bye. When we went in, I saw that in neither of the rooms were the beds undone. It looked like they had slept on the floor and not even touched the blankets, pillows, or towels. I asked them, "What's going on?" They said, "We don't want to cause any problems here." I assured them that the rooms were paid for and that they should use them. They were so respectful. This was just the opposite of what the motel manager had been telling me.

I gave them my Border Angel card and told them to contact me when they left if they had any problems and to see that they were OK. They told us that they really believed in the *angelas de la frontera* (border angels) because when we had met up with them they didn't know what they were going to do.

Three or four months later I got a call from one of the migrants. They had made it to Florida. They told me that they had not had any more problems and that they had found jobs. They thanked me and the Border Angels for our help. This was one of the rare occasions when you hear back from those you have helped. We don't expect this, but it was really good to hear that they were OK.

In the 2009 *Marcha Migrante* we traveled across country and met with various human-rights groups, ending by meeting with policy-makers in Washington, D.C., to try to influence the debate over immigration reform. Along the way we encouraged people to get their elected representatives to pressure for legislative change, which, I thought, was the only real long-term solution to the tragedy of migrant deaths. The *Marcha* took place from February 2 to February 21, 2009, and we traveled from San Diego to Florida and then up the east coast to Washington, D.C. After some travel in Southern California, some of us flew or drove from Los Angeles to Florida, and then we drove up the coast to Washington, D.C., together.

We started our caravan with a nice little send-off from the community, and people came from all over to support it: families, children, students, activists, community and faith leaders from both sides of the border. From there we went to our first stop, which was always the Holtville cemetery in the Imperial Valley. We had about 15 cars arrive, and we did what we always do, which is to have a moment of reflection. I show people the cemetery; many see it for the first time. The entrance is like any other. As soon as you enter, there is a grave of a young man named Francisco. I always stop at that grave first because several years ago when I came I saw some little girls running around. They came up to me because they recognized me from TV. I said, "Where's your mom?" and they showed me. I said we were going to the back of the cemetery to see the graves. "Would you like to join us?" I said, "By the way, who are you paying homage to here?" The mother said, "My little Mexican American baby." I wondered why she would call him that. I looked down at the grave and saw her baby had been born on the fourth of July and had died on Cinco de Mayo. He had only been one year old when he died. His name was Francisco. That happens to be the first grave as you walk into the cemetery. The last grave in the regular part of the cemetery is a grave for a young man named Eric Silva, one of the thousands and thousands of Mexican American soldiers who have died in U.S. wars. There you see a picture of him in his Marine uniform. He was one of the first persons killed in the invasion of Iraq (Mexican Americans have won more medals of honor since 1900 than any other ethnic group in this country).

When you pass the front of the cemetery, you go back and see a bunch of dirt and these bricks that say John Doe or Jane Doe. If it's John Doe it's a man or a little boy, and if it's Jane Doe it's a woman or a little girl that has died crossing the desert or drowned in the canal and they are unidentified. It's a paupers' graveyard. It's all people who are unidentified, and there are some who are identified but nobody has claimed their body. We now go there about every month to pay homage to these people.

That was our first stop on the *Marcha*. The Mexican counsel came out there. Some local people came out there, many for the first time. We really would like to have D.N.A. tests done on these graves because their families don't know if they have died, are imprisoned, or lost. A few years ago there were about 20 people buried in the cemetery. Now there are more than 700. This is the reason we make this our first stop on these marches. We put crosses on the graves. Border Angels volunteers and supporters made crosses for us and we put them there. Some said, *"Ni una muerte más, reforma ya!"* (Not one more death. Reform now!); others said *"no olvidados"* (not forgotten).

From there we went to Yuma, where we spent the night. It was only about an hour away. We spent the night in a Catholic church, and the next morning we had a meeting with some of the local people. There's an organization that had met us out there before. They were very kind and brought us food, and we had a gathering. They shared what was happening with the immigration situation there. We began gathering signatures. On the whole march, we gathered thousands of signatures calling for just and humane immigration reform.

When we got to Coachella, California, again we had had a great reception from El Comité Latino led by Mario Lazcano just as the previous year when we had gone there. They told us that they wanted to do the first-ever protest of I.C.E. (Immigration and Customs Enforcement), the Border Patrol facility, nearby. We went together to the Indio Border Patrol station and did a protest, prayers, and songs. It was very powerful. They were really delighted that we agreed to do it with them there, in solidarity. That evening we had songs, meals, and dance at the church, the mission in Coachella. The next morning, just like they had done the year before, they woke us up very early in the morning, four o'clock, even though we were very tired. They woke us up with *"Las Mañanitas"* sung by mariachis, *tamales*, music, and the community, a *banda*. The mayor of Coachella came and did a whole big event for us. It was incredible. It was beautiful. We really thanked Mario and the organization. They did a fantastic job. They decided to join us for a while.

After *"Las Mañanitas"* and the breakfast, they had a private mass for us. It was beautiful. From there we went to La Placita in Olvera Street in Los Angeles, where we had a very nice event, met with several organizations, and had a press conference with C.O.F.E.M., M.A.P.A., *Hermandad, Casa Refugio*, Maya films, the Mexica movement, and many more. That evening we had a commitment with Cal State University, Long Beach, with Gloria Inzunza, a teacher friend of mine. They had an immigration forum with some of the professors, a Japanese man who spoke about the Japanese experience in internment camps during World War II, a Mexican man who spoke about the importance of education, and some young students talking about the Dream Act and how that was going to influence their future. Then they asked me to speak at the end. I gave some testimonials and an update on our work. I asked Mario from Coachella to speak; he shared with us some hate-crime stories of beatings that had taken place at the hands of the police. Some innocent people had been killed. It was a very powerful presentation, and the students were really into it. Then we had a moment of silence, a vigil, and a meal. Then we continued on our way because we had to get back to San Diego that night, Wednesday, in my case to fly out Thursday to Florida and begin the east coast swing of *Marcha Migrante IV*.

That Friday in Miami, Florida, we went on national Univision radio where we talked about the *Marcha Migrante* and how on this one, in contrast to the first, we were going to Washington, D.C., to galvanize the community along the way, not to march, not to vote, but to lobby for immigration reform. We were telling this administration that now is the time: stop the raids, stop the wall, and give us immigration reform. We had marched; we had voted; now it was time to deliver. The audience was very receptive. We were there in Florida, a state that had gone from red to blue voting for president Barack Obama the previous November.

In Florida, you have people from all over South, Central, and North America, and then some, and many are very well established. It's wonderful. After the radio show, we had a beautiful noon mass. This mass had a lot of community members that came. Then we had a big rally afterwards and did a series of events in Florida that first day. We wanted to spend a lot of time in Florida, three or four days. On each *Marcha* we have targeted one state to spend time in—California on the first

Marcha, Arizona on the second, Texas on the third, and now Florida. We went to an area not too far from Miami where there were these two children from Nicaragua, the Sosa children. One of their parents had been deported because of a raid, and the other parent was in detention. They needed help. We met in solidarity with them and to lend our support. Then that evening we went to Homestead, where we had spent the night, and they had a cook-out and a big event for us. By then our *Marcha* had about 25 automobiles. We gathered another ten cars the next morning. We all went to another community, named Immokalee, where we did some outreach, rallies, and activities with the community. Then we went to Fort Myers, where there are a lot of day laborers, and we met there with them. On the same day we went to Tampa, where we had another community gathering. All during this *Marcha*, as usual, we were gaining more and more community support. It ended that Saturday with a religious service.

Being a Catholic and a Christian, I've been to a lot of services. I've been with rabbis, Sikhs, priests, lay people, and so forth. Never have I had a more powerful religious service than I did that evening in Plant City, Florida. We went to Plant City and met with a Puerto Rican priest, father Carlos, and we did a devotion for two and a half hours. I've never been to a ceremony like this. It wasn't a mass. The priest was very dedicated. There was a lot of prayer. He gave Rita Méndez, a good friend and lead Florida organizer, and me a special blessing.

The next morning we went to Jacksonville, which is up in the north of the state. There we went to another religious service, not Catholic. I think it was Methodist. Lots of the crowd were from Haiti, and I speak a little French so I greeted them. The rest in the congregation were from other Latin American countries. They asked me to speak in French so I said a few words about how we are all the same race, the human race, and so forth. It was a wonderful experience to be with that community in northern Florida, near Jacksonville. (I thought of them right after the January, 2010, earthquake.) Afterwards, we did a rally at a police athletic club facility, and a bunch of Brazilians came. I'll never forget it because while we were there they held up some signs saying, "Brazil supports Border Angels." More of the human race.

Usually when I tell a story I try to relate it to the people whom I'm talking to, so I told the story of a sad case. One day when I was reading the local paper in San Diego, there was the story of a woman named María. She was driving home with her son, a teenager, from work at a local indigenous casino. She was driving on a two-lane road toward her home in Boulevard, California. All of a sudden she saw the lights of a car coming toward her driving on the wrong side of the road. That often happens with these smugglers who try to avoid the checkpoints that are out there. They'll drive down a dirt road and on the other side at 2 or 3 in the morning when there is very little traffic, to avoid the checkpoint. María was driving and saw this oncoming car. She tried to guess which way the car was going to go, so she swerved to the right to protect her son, Mario, who was the passenger. The other car swerved to the left and they met head-on. This was a tragic accident. Several people died, three Brazilians and five Mexicans. I shared this story with the people there because at that time the majority of people coming across, after Mexicans, were Brazilians because their economy was really bad then. I told them about María, who happened to be a Mexican immigrant with documents who had lived here for a long time. I got in touch with María by phone. She knew who I was and about our work, and she asked me to come out there to set up some rescue stations near where she lived. Here was a woman who was a victim of a crime where undocumented immigrants were involved, a lot of people died, and she wanted to help out. She could have been angry, but no, she reached out. To this day we have Border Angel stations in that area.

We left Jacksonville and headed to the next place, Charleston, South Carolina. It's quite a drive. We got to Charleston and met with a woman, a person who this *Marcha* was all about. I had never met her before. I had read an e-mail about her, how she had held a rally to protest against all the raids that had been taking place, and a thousand people came to it. Her name was Diana Salazar. I contacted her, and she invited us to come there. She told us she would take care of lodging and everything. It was a long drive so we got there in the evening. The community was there waiting for us. The majority were Mexican immigrants. They had food and lots of questions. We spent the night in different people's houses in Charleston. The next morning we went to the College of Charleston, and there were these young students and mostly Anglo kids who had come out to San Diego to visit the border with us. We had a forum with them with several teachers and students.

After Charleston we ended up changing our plans because we knew that the next day there was going to be a legislative event for L.U.L.A.C. (League of United Latin American Citizens), the oldest Latino organization in the country. They had invited us to be partners in that conference with them while they discussed legislative business with representatives from the White House, Congress, and Homeland Security. Rosa Rosales, their president, had contacted me and asked me to speak, and I said sure. She is a wonderful leader and good friend. It was a little earlier than we had planned to be in Washington, D.C., but it would work out, so we just took off.

We drove and drove to get to D.C. We had to get there by nine o'clock at night because by nine thirty the church we were going to stay at was going to be locked. We really didn't know what that meant, but when we got there about nine, it was kind of tricky to find this place. It was in a place where the homeless were hanging out, in one of those kinds of communities. We got there before 9:30 and I'm glad because it was a really big church, and if we were locked out there was no way they could hear you. There was nobody inside. It was one of the places used during the presidential inauguration. That's how I knew about it. (I had been invited to Washington for President Obama's inauguration.) I had talked to the priest on the phone, and he was going to let us stay there. They had a guard. We were going to stay three nights but spent only one. We thought maybe we could stay somewhere closer to where the activities were going to be. That one night at the church turned out to be a very powerful experience. We had to get out early the next morning because there was a service going to take place. We slept in the choir loft on the floor and on some of the sofas.

We appreciated being there that one night and then the next morning had to head over to the L.U.L.A.C. conference where there were going to be a lot of prominent people speaking, like Janet Murgía, president of the National Council of la Raza; Frank Sharry with America's Voice; Rosa Rosales with L.U.L.A.C.; and many community members. They asked me to say a few words. It was really a good conference about immigration. They were very gracious. They gave us lunch and let us go to all the forums and speak several times. They offered to put us up at the hotel. There were a lot of us, and a few had relatives in the D.C. area. There was a guy who arrived at the church about eleven o'clock the night before, a student, Carlos, from the award-winning newspaper the *Southwestern Sun* at Southwestern College (in Chula Vista, CA). They have loyally been with us at every *Marcha Migrante*.

The next day we did the legislative visits. I met with David Martin, a top aide who works with Janet Napolitano, head of Homeland Security. I went to their offices and talked a lot about the raids, stopping the wall, Friendship Park, and immigration reform. He was very receptive. He comes from the Migration Policy Institute in Washington, D.C., a very respected research group. We had several visits with Congress people like Congressman Luis Gutierrez, who is to me the leader on the Democratic side of the immigration debate. We met with a congressman, Diaz Ballart, on the Republican side from Florida, who was also pro-immigration, because we wanted to find out what it was that we needed to do to get this bill on the floor and how we could get it passed. We also met with people who were opposed. We didn't want to just meet with people on our side because we would be wasting our time. We divided the group and went and visited legislators on both sides of the aisle and spent the entire day doing that. That evening L.U.L.A.C. had their legislative ball they invited us to; we went, and Senator Bob Menendez was there. He is a leader in the Senate on this immigration debate. The ambassador to Mexico, Arturo Sarukhán, was there, as was Hilda Solis, Secretary of Labor, and Antonio Villaraigosa, the mayor of L.A. I went to say hello to all of them and told them a little bit about what we were doing.

We had about ten cars of people in the *Marcha Migrante* so the next day, on Thursday, February 12, we left for Richmond, Virginia, which was our next stop. That was a long drive as well. When we arrived there was a group waiting for us, and we had a service at a church. Again, it was a Spanish-speaking community. There was a man, Guadencio Fernandez, from Manassas whom I had spoken to on the phone. He had built a wall on his property because he wanted to make a statement about the border wall.[22] He came and gave a talk, and we had a lot of people at that gathering in the church. Guadencio is featured in a movie about his experience. At the church they fed us, and we ended up spending the night with the people from Virigina, mostly Anglos.

The next day, February fourteenth, Valentine's Day, we went to a place in Shenandoah, Pennsylvania, where there had been a horrible hate crime the previous July, 2008. Luis Ramírez had been killed. He was a young Mexican man who had an Anglo girlfriend who was a mother of their children. He was just walking down the street, and three American kids saw him. They were out to kill a Mexican, and they killed him. It was a really tragic case that made international news.

On all of our marches we always hold vigils. The previous year we went up the coast and did a vigil for Cesar Chavez at La Paz, California, where he is buried. This time we did our main vigils on February 14 and 15. One was for Luis Ramírez, right on the spot where he had been killed. They warned us not to go there because there are a lot of K.K.K. and hate groups in the area. The Department of Justice called me. Representatives from the governor's office called me. But I talked to them, and they said they would have a lot of security. The community was really scared to come out. But we went, and there were some local community members. You could feel the tension, the hate. There were several hate guys there, a lot of police, the Department of Justice, the governor's office, a lot of media. We did the prayer vigil, and it was very powerful. I'll never forget. The mayor, the police, and the hate groups were together. After the vigil we even prayed for the three perpetrators of the crime. Why? Because they were not born that way—only love overcomes hate.

---

[22] A film has been made about this memorial wall, called "9500 Liberty."

There's a lot of history in Shenandoah. Over the past four years there have been four migrants who have suspiciously committed suicide there in the jails, all four by hanging themselves with their belts. Two of the four didn't have belts when they went in. They had sweat pants on. They don't like outside people coming in. But I said that because of what happened to Luis Ramírez it was important that we go there. We announced the formation of a new group, the Latino Anti-Discrimination Alliance (L.A.D.A.), because there is no group that looks at hate crimes specifically against Latinos, like the A.D.L., which looks into hate crimes against Jewish people. It is based on the same kind of philosophy only toward Latinos.[23]

The first act was this vigil for Luis Ramírez. God is great. I don't believe in coincidences. Afterward, we went to have a meal in a restaurant. During the meal someone overheard us and said, "You know who owns this restaurant? The family of Luis Ramírez." I met the uncle and aunt. They told us how grateful the whole community was, but that they couldn't go because they would suffer the consequences. They said, "We're glad you selected this restaurant," thinking that we did it because we knew who owned it. There are not very many Mexican restaurants in Shenandoah. We had people from Border Angels who met us there. They were from Philadelphia. There was a young woman named Pat, who was very pro-Border Angels, who had met with me in San Diego several times. She drove two hours to meet us there. We had a guy named Dr. Gonzales from Hazleton, Pennsylvania. He was from the governor's office. He helped us a lot in Shenandoah. He invited us to Hazleton to spend the night, but we refused because the mayor of that town is very racist, and we didn't want to give any support to them. We drove and drove that night, arriving in New York, and spent the night in our cars. It was about 20 degrees, very cold.

We went to New York City and then to Long Island where we did a vigil for Marcelo Lucero, who was killed by a group of seven "good" kids who had decided they wanted to have a "beaner boot party." They found a young man walking along the street in a small town near Farmingville, Long Island, New York, and they kicked him to death. It ended up he wasn't Mexican but Ecuadorian. Marcelo Lucero died tragically, and we did a prayer vigil there. That was Sunday, February 15, and I picked up the local paper because I wanted to find out what was going on in general and keep in the spirit of the community. It said that Marcelo Lucero's mom was coming from Ecuador. She was flying in on Tuesday. I said, "We're staying for a couple of days." We were

---

[23] L.A.D.A. is now part of *Gente Unida*.

supposed to be in Washington that day. We made all our decisions by consensus. Marcelo's family flew in, and we had a service for them that night. The mother wasn't feeling well and couldn't attend, but his sister did and I sat with her. They really need help in that community. The largest Latino community they have is Ecuadorian. They told us the same thing that we had heard in Shenandoah, that the crimes were not unexpected. There had been violence leading up to that. The trial in New York started that week, which is why the mom and daughter had flown in. I told them that we would keep an eye on it. The L.A.D.A. is going to play a role in it.

On February seventeenth there was going to be a religious event at the church on Long Island so during the day in New York City we went to the C.N.N. headquarters where we had been the previous day, but they had been closed because it was President's Day. We went back, and I hand-delivered a letter to Jonathan Kline, who was the president of C.N.N. The Border Angels had been advocating for the firing of Lou Dobbs since 2005. In the letter I said, "You've got to let Lou Dobbs go. Because of Lou Dobbs people are inspired to do what we had experienced last week, as well as the people who had killed Luis Ramirez and Marcelo Lucero. I'm sure you're going to say there's no relation, but there is." In November of 2009, because of growing national pressure from the Border Angels and other groups, C.N.N. fired Dobbs.

I firmly believe, without a doubt, that when Lou Dobbs, Roger Hedgecock, Bill O'Reilly, Rick Roberts (all conservative talk-show hosts), and other people like them across the country do what they do, it leads to an escalation of hate crimes like what happened to Luis Ramírez and Marcelo Lucero. There are other groups that have organized boycotts of the programs like Rush Limbaugh's, and we've supported that. But you have to be really organized on that.

Afterward we went back to Washington, D.C., and continued with our originally planned meetings with policy-makers. On February eighteenth, we met with key people. In my case I met with the staffs of Senator Kyle, Congressman Zole Laughrin, Senator Mark Warner, Senator Bob Melendez, Harry Reid, and others. On the seventeenth, when we arrived in D.C., we stayed at a woman's house, the cousin of one of the women who was with us from Illinois. Her name was Arlene Limas, and she had a tae kwon do studio. I used to do a little of that. We went to a huge studio that night at about three in the morning. We slept on the mats. I looked on the walls and saw some gold medals for tae kwon do won in the Olympics in Korea in 1988. To win that sport in the country that had invented it, Arlene must have been awesome, and she was. We met her the next morning, and she said, "No, no, you're not staying here. You're staying at my house." We stayed with her a couple of days. She was wonderful. We have had incredible people on all seven *Marcha Migrantes*.[24]

We did all these visits on the hill February eighteenth and nineteenth, and on February nineteenth we met with Juan Hernández, whom I had met several years before. He's McCain's main Latino strategist and had worked with Mexican President Fox. We talked, and said we needed a meeting of about a dozen people in Congress, six from each side of the aisle, and not to advertise this meeting, but just to talk about how we were going to get this done. I already had six people, and he was going to get six people from his side, including some evangelical leaders, who were very important. Juan said that he wanted to get this immigration bill done. Even though Juan and I are on different sides of the aisle politically, we are on the same side with respect to the immigration issue. *Fortune Magazine* once called him one of the 100 smartest people in the world. He is a regular on national media and a good friend.

We also had meetings with the staff of Senator James Clayborne, and we met with some of the judicial committee members who are very important on immigration. We also met about the much needed investigation of sheriff Joe Arpaio in Arizona. Then we had a meeting in the office of Congressman Luiz Gutierrez. Perhaps the most powerful meeting we had was with the Hispanic working group. Some of them have come to the border before and met with me. These are the Latino staff of the legislators. They are representatives from all the legislators' offices; they were all Latino Democrats very familiar with this issue, and they were moved by the stories we told about the migrants. We had some strong allies there because these people were the gatekeepers. The decision-makers were their bosses, but they were the gatekeepers. I wanted to invite all of them to the border to see what was happening, because these kids were the future congress people. They were the brightest kids in their school.

The next day, February twentieth, we started heading back. I stayed an extra day because I was going to fly back to San Diego for a commitment to have a prayer vigil at Friendship Park. On the twentieth I met with some national organizations to see how we could partner up. I met with the National Immigration Forum, with America's Voice, and with the Migration Policy Institute, where the two former heads of the I.N.S. now work. Then I flew back to San Diego to be at the Friendship

---

[24] As this second edition goes to press in the Summer of 2015, there have now been 10 Marcha Migrantes.

Park event on the twenty-first. That was kind of an exclamation point on what we had done.

The main lessons we learned from this cross-country *Marcha Migrante* were how we share so much with other communities far from San Diego. Wherever we went the people all responded very positively and gave us tremendous support. We motivated one another to go further in the struggle. Despite our ragged appearance, the contacts we made in Washington, D.C., were valuable. However, as is true in much of life, only the future will tell of the consequences. Still, it was a good beginning.

The grassroots basis of all this travel and organizing was the Border Angels organization in San Diego. Our main mission has been to stop the deaths in the desert, and changing the immigration laws is the most effective way to do this. Since the 1990s, the construction of multiple border walls has forced thousands of immigrants to cross the desert in Arizona and elsewhere. For us, the wall is a symbol of what is wrong with our country's immigration policies. That's why the issue of Friendship Park is very important to all those concerned with human rights.

The U.S. side of "Friendship Park."

Chapter 7

Friendship Park

Friendship Park is located in the southwesternmost portion of the United States. It is located within Border Field State Park. Here is where they began construction of the new border fencing, double walls and triple walls in some places, separated by a no man's land and patrolled by Border Patrol officers on A.T.V.s.

In 1971, First Lady Patricia Nixon went there, inaugurated this park, and said, "May there never be a fence between these two great nations so that people can extend a hand in friendship." For decades people have been going to that area and crossing to the other side. If they went north they came to Imperial Beach in San Diego and played soccer, or if they went south they would go into Playas de Tijuana to eat some tacos. This went on for generations, and this was Friendship Park. It was an international zone where families could get together for picnics and to enjoy the beach.

Before they built a new security zone in Friendship Park, I went there with a group from *"Despierta América"* (Univisión's national morning show), and, sure enough, there was a family gathered on both sides of the wall. The father on the U.S. side didn't have his papers to be able to cross into Mexico and reenter the U.S. His wife didn't have the documentation to come to the United States. The wife's entire family was on one side, and the father had driven down from Los Angeles. It was very moving. They were crying and upset that they were going to close the park, and they wouldn't be able to meet like this any more. The mother brought the baby up to the wall so the father could kiss it through the partition in the wall. That human contact is what Friendship Park has now lost. The new wall and cages that they have built make it impossible for human contact. Before the new fencing, somebody told me that they had seen a couple who courted each other on opposite sides of the wall, the boy on the U.S. side and the girl on the Mexican side. They talked through the wall. The couple had met through a mutual friend, and the only physical contact they had was through the wall at Friendship Park. Eventually, they fell in love, and he gave her the ring through the wall. He couldn't cross to do this because if he did he wouldn't be able to come back. They got married. Now people travel long distances from all over the country to Friendship Park, not knowing that the fencing makes it impossible for them to meet their loved ones, or they will arrive to find that the Border Patrol has closed the area down. Their relatives on the Mexican side wonder what happened to their loved ones. We really need to reopen Friendship Park.

Right at the beginning of the wall is the Pacific Ocean, and the wall actually goes into the ocean for 20-30 yards. As you go up the hill from the ocean, there is a monument that commemorates when the United States invaded Mexico and stole half its territory. The Treaty of Guadalupe Hidalgo was signed on February 2, 1848, and there's a monument there on what is the dividing line between the United States and Mexico. This is a place that we call Friendship Park. The Border Patrol calls the whole area Border Field State Park, and the area where we meet they call Friendship Circle.

Sadly, when they suddenly put the wall right in the middle of Friendship Park you couldn't cross from one side to the other. They built a small area near the monument and allowed only 25-30 people at a time to go there after traveling though a corridor and second gate. People are no longer allowed to touch or get close to one another. Roberto Martinez, who I call the father of Friendship Park, started doing something called *Posada Sin Fronteras* the very first year of Operation Gatekeeper in 1994. He decided that on the Saturday closest to Christmas we would gather on both sides of the border and have a *Posada Sin Fronteras* based on a very old Mexican celebration where people would reenact the story of Joseph and Mary looking for a place to give birth to Jesus as they traveled from house to house seeking shelter. All they heard was, "There's no room at the inn" until they found lodging (*posada*) in a barn, and Jesus was born. Participants sing songs, have special bread, and have a celebration, which includes lots of foods and a piñata for the children. It's a beautiful celebration with people on both sides of the border. Various community organizations and religious groups meet, do an enactment of the *Posada*, and have hot chocolate, tamales, sing songs, and throw candies across the wall. The traditional *Posada* is a whole series of songs. They usually start 12 days before Christmas. We have the church involved, community members, and for most of the years we've done it at Friendship Park, although there have been a couple of times that we've done it in another area, when there is too much rain—over by the gate, which is now called Roberto's Gate, just east of the San Ysidro Port of Entry. Now we can no longer even do that because they closed that area off as well.

For most of the history of *La Posada Sin Fronteras* we've been involved as one of the organizers, along with Interfaith Committee, *Casa Migrante* from Tijuana, American Friends Service Committee, people from the *Casa Asunta* in Tijuana, Mexico's Human Rights Commission, and others. We've had people from both sides of the border who have gotten together to do the planning. We've done a lot of events. The Border Angels are one of the most active organizations there. For about six years, until 2010, we would do events there maybe once a month. It might be a mass, communion, or a prayer vigil. It might be the making of an altar on both sides of the border. There were other groups involved as well. Another group active on a regular basis has been the Border Encuentro, formerly called "Make Friends Not Fences." The group is active every month. Now you can no longer gather at Friendship Park because they put extra fencing there. The families can no longer go right up to the wall and put their fingers through to touch their grandchild for the first time or share a meal.

When they closed Friendship Park in 2008 a half a dozen of us formed a group, Friends of Friendship Park. Because of the secure fence act signed by President Bush, people were no longer able to meet as they had before, so we formed this committee to make sure that we reopened Friendship Park.

I've gone back to Washington, D.C., several times on my own to talk to some of the key people about reopening Friendship Park. I've gotten a lot of support from some people in the Departement of Homeland Security (D.H.S.) and other departments. The Friends of Friendship Park meets about once a month now to talk about the strategy. I've met with some friends from both sides of the border, and we came up with a model of what we wanted the reopening of the park to look like. It was loosely based on Friendship Arch on the Canadian border. I took the plan to Washington, D.C., and when I met with Alan Bersin after he became the border czar for the second time I said, "You've got to show us a newer and kinder Alan Bersin because one of the great things that the Obama Administration could do would be to reopen Friendship Park." He said, "It's not up to me. I want this decision to be made by the local Border Patrol chief, Mike Fisher." We walked out of the meeting. Mike Fisher was right there. Bersin said, " I want you to meet with Enrique." We set up a one-on-one meeting, and Mike said, "Let's do it. Let's reopen it." I told some of the Friends of Friendship Park, "See, they're open to it. Let's get going."[25] I agree that we have to work as a committee, and we, as a committee, continue to work on reopening Friendship Park. I and others have met with the authorities to lobby for a more humane, a kinder, gentler Friendship Park. The results so far have not been what we are looking for, but I am absolutely convinced we will succeed. Maybe the *Posada* will be down on the beach this year, as long as families can gather on both sides.

---

[25]Since then there have been two Border Patrol chiefs succeeding Fisher.

One of the things that I've learned from Roberto Martinez is the power of communication and of talking to people. I know that with the new Alan Bersin, you do see a change. As an example, when I met with Alan; he was coming to San Diego two months later, in May, and having two community forums, one at the Catfish Club (an African American organization) and one was at the Institute of the Americas at U.C.S.D. I told him I would be there, but I had to call him to say that I couldn't attend because Roberto Martinez had passed away, and I had to help organize Roberto's services. I asked Alan to mention the passing of Roberto Martinez in his talks, which he did. This was evidence of the new and improved Alan Bersin. In order to have change you need to work with both sides.

The events that I will always remember at Friendship Park are the masses that we used to hold. We have a picture on the website of Fr. Henry on one side of the fence and on the other side Fr. Luis, the priest who runs Tijuana's *Casa Migrante*. It was beautiful. We would have two altars set up on their respective sides of the fence, and we would pass communion through the fence. Fr. Henry would give communion to those on the Mexican side and Fr. Luis to those on the U.S. side. To me it was very significant; this kind of love and spirituality has no border. We demonstrated that. We still do those kinds of things, except we can't do them at Friendship Park. Now we can't go anywhere along the fence there. Often we would have music, singing, prayers, and poetry on both sides of the fence on a regular basis. Sometimes there would be a protest of somebody's deportation. We had building of altars on the Day of the Dead on both sides of the fence. We would put crosses on the fence. When we have the *Marcha Migrantes* we start or end at Friendship Park. When we came back from the first *Marcha* on February 28, 2006, we ended it on the Mexican side of Friendship Park. On *Marcha Migrante II* we ended it at Friendship Park, and then we had a town hall in San Ysidro to talk about immigration and the stories we had gathered.

On *Marcha Migrante III, Su Voto es Su Voz* in 2008, we went all the way to the Canadian border where we were supposed to meet Elvira Arellano, the most famous of all the deportees, after she had been taking refuge in a church in Chicago for a year because she didn't want to be separated from her son, Saul. I had asked her to meet us at the Canadian border at a place they call Friendship Arch. That's the kind of space we want here on the San Diego border. There in Canada people can cross openly near Vancouver to the U.S., just like they used to do in Friendship Park. They have cameras and the Border Patrol there just like here, but they let you cross and make sure that you cross back. That's the kind of thing that we are working for.

On this historic Border Angels Children's Day Celebration—April 28, 2013—the door between San Diego and Tijuana was opened for the first time ever. We watch, as 5-year-old Ximena hugs her father, Luis René, for the first time ever.

Elvira called me from the airport in Vancouver and told me that they would not let her out of the airport because they knew we were there in the Friendship Arch area. I was really upset. We had lots of people waiting to meet her. I told her, "Elvira, go back to Tijuana and meet me on the Mexican side at Friendship Park." When we came back, on February 17, 2008, it was the biggest event ever in the history of Friendship Park. There were almost 3,000 people there on the Mexican side. Elvira was there. When I turned the corner to walk to the park down the beach toward the fence because the roads had been closed for some time I said, "What's that over there?" It was a sea of people on the Mexican side, a marching band, ladders on the fence. It was crazy. It brought tears to my eyes, and Elvira was overwhelmed. That was actually the beginning of the end of Friendship Park because the very next week the Border Patrol began having a checkpoint to enter the park. The week before we had had about 300 people from *Marcha Migrante*, on the U.S. side, who had gone to the fence to meet Elvira. The State Park's official was all worked up and said, "What's going on? You didn't have a permit for this." I said, "I didn't know that all these people would show up." As we were heading back to our cars and walking along the beach, a Border Patrol guy named Officer Miranda stopped me and said, "Enrique, you said you had about 200 people. Well, now you have 206." I knew what he meant. Some six people had jumped over the border fence and mixed in with our group. I asked him, "What are you going to do?" and he said, "Well, I'm going to check everybody's IDs." For me that was a concern for various reasons, so I told him, "Lots of these people were with me on the *Marcha Migrante*, and some of them might not have their IDs with them now." He said, "If you can convince these six people to go back, I won't check any IDs." I spoke to the group, and I saw the six persons mixed in with our group. They were carrying crosses, just young kids. I had been on the road for two and a half weeks, and I knew exactly who was in our group. But I didn't look directly at them. A few other people had just joined us from San Diego. I said, "I know there are a few extra people in the group. You are more than welcome to be with us. I'm glad you came. But now is not the time to enter further into the United States. You see that agent over there? Well, as soon as we leave here he is going to check everyone's IDs. For those of you who have just joined us, who may have joined us from the Mexican side, God bless you, and I hope you have success some other time, but now is not the time to cross. Today is not the day. I would really appreciate it if you would walk back." These six kids gave me their crosses, and they went back. The Border Patrol didn't do anything to them. They had squeezed between the tubes down by the water.

After *Marcha Migrante IV* we walked into Friendship Park with the Friends of Friendship Park and we had music. Unfortunately, the Minutemen also joined us, and there was almost violence because of their provocation, but as usual they were a very small group and were ignored. When I talked to Alan Bersin, I told him, "You cannot allow these Minutemen to go down there. They are provoking. They are very aggressive. We have little kids with us. We have the San Diego musicians with us. They are harrassing. That's not acceptable."

Friendship Park is to me a very special place. Society is judged by how they treat their children, and that's a place where grandchildren meet their grandparents for the first time. I remember once when I was there just before they shut it down, a man from Guadalajara who had not seen his wife in ten years met her through the fence then. They were talking and she had her little baby, their nephews, too. I, too, know this family. It was a wonderful thing to see. I am confident that the park will reopen, and I will not stop until it does.

The struggle surrounding Friendship Park has taught us how recognizing a shared sense of community and culture is important in the immigration debate. The fencing, military-like policing, and the restrictive laws divide families and communities and do not promote the best that is America. The sentiments engraved on the Statue of Liberty should also apply to our southern border:

> Give me your tired, your poor,
> Your huddled masses yearning to breathe free,
> The wretched refuse of your teeming shore.
> Send these, the homeless, tempest-tossed to me.
> I lift my lamp beside the golden door.[26]

Since the first edition of this book, Friendship Park is now open on weekends thanks to the work of the Friends of Friendship Park, with architect, Jim Brown, Reverand John Fanestil, myself, and others.

---

[26]Emma Lazarus, "The New Colossus," engraved on the pedestal of the Statue of Liberty.

Chapter 8

Water in the Desert

Five men stumbled out of the mountain pass so sunstruck they didn't know their own names, couldn't remember where they'd come from, had forgotten how long they'd been lost. One of them wandered up a peak. One of them was barefoot. They were burned nearly black, their lips huge and cracking, what a paltry drool still available to them spuming from their mouths in a salty foam as they walked. Their eyes were cloudy with dust almost too dry to blink up a tear. Their hair was hard and stiffened by old sweat, standing in crowns from their scalps, old sweat because their bodies were no longer sweating. They were drunk from having their brains baked in the pan, they were seeing God and devils, and they were dizzy from drinking their own urine, the poisons clogging their systems.[27]

This opening account by Luis Urrea of migrants crossing the Sonoran desert gives us a vivid picture of what it is like to be lost and dying of heat prostration and thirst. Urrea's account is based on a true story of how 14 people died in Arizona crossing into the U.S. in May, 2001. It is a tragedy that is reenacted every summer in the deserts of the Southwest.

The Border Angels was formed to help these migrants in trouble. Specifically, we were originally known for our mission of leaving water in the desert for migrants during the summer. I first started hearing about the dramatic rise in immigrant deaths in 1995 and, with some other people, we started trying to do something about it. Back then the place where most people were crossing from Mexico to the U.S. was in the Imperial Valley. The deaths went from one or two a month to one a day. You started reading in the paper that a body was found in the Imperial Valley, or in East San Diego County, Boulevard, Potrero, and all these different areas east of San Diego. While the Border Angels continued efforts in the canyons, with water and food there, occasionally we would go out to the desert and put out water, but it wasn't in an organized manner. In 1996, I would just drive out there, maybe for a meeting or an occasion, and leave water. We would leave water by the tall, high-voltage transmission towers, which is a natural place for people to go. Other people were doing the same thing, but it was not an organized effort.

---

[27]Luis Alberto Urrea, *The Devil's Highway: A True Story* (New York: Little Brown and Co., 2004), p. 3.

In 2000, I heard about a guy in Calexico who had a plan to put water out in the desert. He turned out to be John Hunter, Duncan Hunter's brother (Duncan Hunter was a conservative Republican Congressman whose district includes East County). At first I was very suspicious because Duncan Hunter was largely responsible for supporting the policies that had led to thousands of border deaths. He had been the number-one advocate for Operation Gatekeeper. His brother, John Hunter, began distributing water in the spring of 2000, and in the summer of 2001 I met him. I remember he was attending a monthly breakfast in Barrio Logan at Chuey's Restaurant (the San Diego Latina/o and Indigenous Unity Coalition monthly breakfasts). He was introduced as needing volunteers for his water project. After the meeting I talked to him and told him about our work in the canyons and how we also left water. He said that he had met some guy in Calexico who wanted to put flags up to help the immigrants find the water. I thought that was a good idea so we joined forces. He called his organization Water Stations and later, when we joined forces, Water/Winter Stations. He incorporated it as a non-profit group, and they elected me the president. Soon this group really grew. We had blue flags out there and boxes for the water. The reason he had gone to the Unity Coalition breakfast was that he didn't have many volunteers. I was with the Padres and being an activist I was able to bring a lot of volunteers. We really expanded the organization and eventually had several hundred water stations. We had a board of directors with people like Oscar Naranjo and David Pino, both of whom had known me before from my work with the House of Mexico, another organization I had founded. We raised a lot of money.

As a result of *Sábado Gigante* and some ideological differences we formalized a much larger group called Border Angels in 2002. Soon there were other groups along the border doing the same thing, leaving water for migrants, especially in Arizona, No More Deaths and Humane Border, for example. We would go out there and put water at their stations, too. It isn't about who gets credit. It's about saving lives.

Finally, we formed our own non-profit group, and we started putting our own orange flags out, going further into the desert where you need four-wheel drive vehicles. We also started going to the other side of the border to put out water and working with a Mexican group called *Grupo Beta*. We continued going out to the Imperial Valley in the summers when the temperature routinely reaches 120 degrees Fahrenheit. What happened was that in 2001 and 2002 people who lived in the Imperial Valley started seeing what we were doing, and they would call me and say, "I want you to put water on my land." Today we have a lot of water stations on private land. One guy who used to be a teacher at Chula Vista High School, Mr. Davalos, had about 40 acres where he let us put seven or eight stations. Recently we got a call from a lady who owns land right on the border, and she wanted us to put water on her land.

Up until 9/11, the number-one place where people have crossed was Imperial Valley. Now it's shifted out to Arizona where we started working with other groups and other people. There are also several groups in Texas, which now is a major place for people to cross. I told them you have to know your area because each one is unique. Here in San Diego we have mountains, and it's a little different from the desert. In Texas you have the Rio Grande. But there are groups trying to prevent deaths on both sides of the border. We're one of the groups that works on both sides of the border.

When we go to the Mexican side of the border we work with *Grupo Beta*, which is like the Red Cross, a search and rescue operation. They started about the same time as we did, seeing the tremendous increase in the desert deaths in 1996. What they do is drive out into the desert in four-wheel vehicles, see people walking, come up and ask if they are OK, and get their names. They won't tell them that they can't cross, but they ask the names in case something happens to them. They'll tell them, "It's very dangerous to be walking out here, and a lot of things can happen. If you want, we can give you a ride back to Mexicali or Tecate or wherever."

Grupo Beta is all along the northern border from Tijuana to Matamoros as well as the southern border with Guatemala. What we do is contact them. We'll be going with them in September when it's really hot. We'll meet with them in Mexicali, for example, go to their offices, and then we'll hop in their trucks and go into the desert. We'll do very similar work as on the U.S. side. We'll put up the flags, with iron rebar, and leave the water with the big orange flag. The difference in working with them rather than on the U.S. side is that in the U.S. we sometimes have to work with government agencies. When we go into the mountains sometimes a forest ranger will go with us because of the mountain lions and other dangers.

One ranger was a Czechoslovakian guy who went with us when we were putting up the winter stations with blankets and food. Once he said, "Enrique, come here. I want to show you something." It was a CD with a Czechoslovakian mariachi group on it. He was playing the music, and was really proud. I had met him originally because the Forest Service was concerned with fire danger from migrants. His name was Mike, and he told me his story, how he had been in the Marines and how his family had crossed from eastern to western Europe. He was thinking of his family and how they had had to flee the Nazis as undocumented immigrants. He became a very strong supporter.

The water project evolved from the canyons in 1986, and we started to see the need for leaving water in the desert. As I said, other groups did the same thing. Of them all, No More Deaths is my favorite. They do incredible work. All of us were working on the same things. Even before these groups, people from the Imperial Valley were leaving water because they live out there and they know the need. This was even before Operation Gatekeeper.

Basically, our operations runs like this: we meet at a strategic area. Some of the people who come to work with us don't have cars, and they come from out of town by public transportation. In Pantoja Park there's a statue of the former president of Mexico, Benito Juárez, one of the indigenous heroes of the Americas, who stands for respect and human rights. We meet at his statue, and we give a little talk. I tell them a little bit about Border Angels, and they tell me who they are. I tell them what we are going to do that day.[28] Sometimes we go to visit the day laborers and bring them water, or we go to the canyons or mountains or deserts. When we go to work on the water project, because of the funding situation, I ask everyone to bring three to five gallons of water. I ask them to wear sturdy shoes because we are going to be out in the desert where there are scorpions, snakes, and things like that. I ask them to bring sun block and wear a baseball cap.

We meet and caravan in cars out to the Imperial Valley, which is about two hours away. Along the way we stop at spots where we have been leaving water. At some of the spots we've been leaving water for ten years or so. Some are natural areas by the side of the road, and you can tell immigrants have been there. Sometimes you see empty cans of tuna and empty water bottles. We'll stop, leave up to 12 gallons of water, and put up some kind of sign. It might be a cross, a reflector spotlight, a flag, or a combination of all three. The spotlights are usually the lights you have for bicycles. We put them there because a lot of these people are crossing at night. I sometimes put little "Know your rights" cards from the Mexican consulate or from the Border Angels in conjunction with the Human Rights Commission of Mexico. We put those there so that the people will know their rights, and they have emergency numbers.

The numbers of volunteers vary. I've had groups as small as three or four people, and the largest group was almost 60, which is too big, because we will finish leaving the water in a few minutes. The average size is 20 or 30. We divide the group into cars with four or five to a car.

---

[28] Since the first edition of this book, the Border Angels have continued to grow and now have a small office in the Sherman Heights Community Center, San Diego, CA.

Then we hopscotch. The first car goes to a station, and the next car passes it up and goes to the next one, and so forth. You just go as far as you can see cars parked by the side of the road. When we go to Mexicali, the *Grupo Beta* people meet us at the border, and then we go to their offices. We go in their vehicles. We want to do more because I've been working with the agencies on both sides to get them to do it all along the border. On the U.S. side, I've been working with the authorities to have more emergency phones installed along the most desolate parts of the highway 98 between Ocotillo and Yuma. We will put the water near there. They do have radiator water in some areas, such as when you're going up the grade from the Imperial Valley, but the water's really dirty and has lots of bees and garbage.

Another thing that we do when we go out to the Imperial Valley is to go to the cemetery in Holtville just north of Calexico. Sometimes I'll ask groups that are coming to make some crosses out of small pieces of light wood and glue. You'll see crosses made by college and high school groups, or you can see crosses made by Judith Baca, a friend who is an artist from Los Angeles.

The other day I was very disappointed to see a book about the Imperial Valley where the author commented on the gravesites, saying that these illegal aliens are stealing our taxes. I was outraged. They do pay taxes. I intend to reach this author and let him know how inappropriate his statement was. He's got to take it back.

Sometimes in the desert, the water containers have been cut or tampered with, and if we see that the water level is low, I tell the volunteers to dump it out on a plant and we put a new container there. We can tell that they have been used because you'll see a bunch of empty rings from the top of the plastic bottle where they've opened it, and the water's missing. We go through thousands of containers every year.

There have been other incidents involving confrontations with the Minutemen on these trips. In 2005, we were with *Gente Unida* in the desert near Campo from July sixteenth until mid-October every single night camping out to protest the Minutemen, who were also camped out trying to be sort of a vigilante Border Patrol. There were only two people who were there every night during that period, Micaela Saucedo, who runs *Casa de Refugio Migrante* in Tijuana, and Vicente Rodríguez, two very good friends of mine. They have been on all the *Marcha Migrantes*. I would spend the night about once a week, but I would be there every day. There were some real security concerns. We ended up having several hundred people there every night at the beginning. My being there would be a security risk to them. The Minutemen could identify me. I had bumper stickers like "Viva Aztlán!" which would drive them crazy.

That July 16, 2005, the Minutemen arrived in Campo, but we had arrived the day before. That spring I had initiated *Gente Unida*. When the Minutemen arrived, they were stunned to see us there. We had hundreds of people waiting for them, and they had said they were going to have 800 people, but they ended up having only about fifty. They had to camp about a half a mile away. We did a lot of actions against them. We would ride up and down right where they were with megaphones at night. I played my Santana CD, and other people had their music, and we hit them with spotlights. We would broadcast, "*Hermanos migrantes, aquí están unos racistas, los Minutemen. No crucen aquí.*" (Brother migrants, the racist Minutemen are here. Don't cross here.) The Minutemen were furious.

We ruined it for them because from July 16 to October 31 they were there and so were we. On their website they said that their tactic was to say "*buenas noches*" as if that were to say they were not racists and to get the migrants to come closer. The night after we arrived on July 16, we had some young students who had megaphones, spotlights, and boom boxes. They snuck up on them and on a signal shouted out "*Buenas noches*" and put a spotlight on them. The Minutemen jumped up and were all scared. It took them a couple of minutes to realize that these were not migrants but our group. They began chasing the kids back to our campsite, and then they stopped because we had so many people there. This was the beginning of the end of the Minutemen.

When the Minutemen first arrived on July 16 they met at a V.F.W. post. Jim Gilchrist and Jim Chase, the co-founders, were there. We went outside and had a huge crowd that surrounded the V.F.W. lodge, and we chanted, "Racists, go home! Racists, go home!" The sheriff and Border Patrol officers were there and just made sure no one crossed over the line. In one of the videos we have of all this, Jim Gilchrist had a little gas-operated siren that was pretty loud. One of our student supporters also had one, and they were both blasting away, just like little kids. Sometimes at the rescue stations, the Minutemen sabotaged the water bottles. For example, early during the water program, a producer from the "Today Show" was with me, along with the cameraman. The very first water station we went to had a little note addressed to me. It was attached to a water bottle that was different from our bottles. The note said, "There's poison in this bottle, and I hope Enrique Morones drinks it." It turned out not to be poison. Since then, whenever there is a little hole or anything in the bottles we empty them, because nobody is going to do an autopsy of an immigrant found dead of "dehydration" in the desert.

Generoso and Cristauria assist as we take
down the chapel in the canyons.

National Politics

Of course the real solution to the deaths in the desert will come from the U.S. and Mexican governments and their changed policies regarding immigration. For that reason the Border Angels and other human-rights groups also have gotten involved in social justice. To further the cause of a just immigration policy, we have joined with others as individuals and as an organization. The one political campaign that I had worked on before Obama's presidential bid was the Al Gore campaign in 2000. I was involved making phone calls and contacts, speaking on the radio, activities of this kind. With Obama it was really different. First of all, I was really upset in 2000 when the real winner (Al Gore) was not in the White House. In 2008 I was really worried that it would happen again. We had been involved with millions of people in the marches and demonstrations, and people asked how we were going to make a change. I and a lot of other people argued that it would be by having the right person in office who would work on humane immigration reform. My candidate, the person I liked the best and whom I had had on my radio show, was Dennis Kucinich. But he was not a realistic contender. I agreed with a lot of his ideas. I'll never forget that when I had him on my show it was in Spanish, and I said, "Don't worry. I can translate." He said, "I can speak Spanish." The former Mayor of Cleveland? Well, he had taken Spanish in high school, and he did OK. But in 2008 the country was not ready for an idealistic person like him. You were wasting your vote. Among the Democrats, the candidate I liked was Barack Obama. I read his book, and I liked what he had to say. He had sympathy for undocumented persons and even had a relative who was undocumented. He was very charismatic, brilliant, and as a person of color he knew what it was like to suffer the slings and arrows of racism. I started seeing what I could do to get involved. There were rallies and different events here in San Diego. His sister, Maya, came to San Diego, and I met her. I got involved with different efforts, canvassing, phone banking, and meetings. Wherever I would go I would informally bring up the Obama campaign.

I knew of a man named Cuauhtémoc Figueroa, who was the national spokesperson for Barack Obama's Spanish-language effort. I met with him and told him that I had a big following and that I could help. I suggested that I could speak on national media on issues like the Border Angels and immigration, as I had been doing, and bring up that a way to stop the deaths was to have a pathway to legalization, and the best way to do that is to elect Barack Obama. We had the *Marcha Migrante III* in February, 2008, when we traveled from the Friendship Park all the way to the Canadian border, passing through the six western states with the message, *"Tu voto es tu voz"* (Your vote is your voice). I didn't tell them who to vote for, but we all had blue tee shirts. We just wanted people to register to vote. I also started doing all these national shows, speaking at the National Council of La Raza and the League of United Latin American Citizens, and I would meet up with people involved with the campaign. I would share what I was doing. I went with a group to Las Vegas to register voters. I went to Colorado, met with the United Farm Worker people, and we canvassed, going from door to door in Denver. I spoke on the local media in Spanish wherever I went. I participated in debates on immigration reform in Wisconsin and Pennsylvania, and I would spread the word, especially to communities of color, about the need to get Obama elected. I logged 35,000 miles driving and flying all over the country (using my frequent-flyer miles). I was invited to speak at the pre-rally of the Democratic National Convention in Denver as a closing speaker. I told them I was going to be debating Tom Tancredo, a noted conservative opponent of immigration reform, before the big acceptance speech by Barack Obama at Invesco Field. In Denver, Tancredo never showed up, but I told the audience how we needed to stop the deaths and bring about humane immigration reform.

Back in San Diego I would use every occasion when I was invited to speak in the community about the importance of registering to vote. People would literally come up to me and ask me, "Who should I vote for?" I would say, "You shouldn't do that because there are going to be Latinos and others who will vote for a person for the wrong reasons. You should vote for the person who is speaking for you and agrees with your concerns. Your issue might be health care or the economy or whatever. But ideally you should not have only one issue of concern."

The one thing that influenced me tremendously, a life-changing event, was one time when I was working with a volunteer in the desert. She was wondering if it was worthwhile. She was having a hard time. She just lost her job, and she was really involved in the movement. I told her that the one incident that had inspired me was a time I was in the desert and there was a shape in the distance that I thought was one man, but it ended up being two, as one (Francisco) was carrying the other man (Pedro). I went running out there, and they were both really thirsty. One was almost dead. We gave them water and shade right away. I was going to take one of them to the hospital in Calexico, but they didn't want to go. I gave them a couple of minutes to recuperate. We stayed with them for three or four hours in the shade and gave them food and water, and I let them use my phone. After a while we had to go. They asked, "Where are you going?" I said, "We have to go put more water out. You seem to be OK." Well, two weeks later I get a phone call from a little boy, who said, "Hi, sir, you don't know me. My name is Francisco, and I live in Los Angeles. I want to thank you for saving my dad's life." I said, "Wow, that's great! How's your dad do-ing?" "He's fine. He had gone to Mexico because of a family death." I said, "How about Pedro, the other man?" He said, "Pedro, who's that?" I said, "Your dad was carrying somebody on his back. Not only was he coming back to be with you, but he was helping a stranger." I thought of the modesty, values, and courage of this man. That's the kind of man I want to marry my daughter or to be my next-door neighbor. This is the kind of guy that the right-wing nuts are labeling as a terrorist. They could teach me something about values.

Well, two weeks later I get another call, this one from Chicago, and it was the son of Pedro calling to thank me. It was the same thing. When people say it doesn't make a difference, I have to believe it made a difference to people like Francisco and Pedro. When I speak to stu-dents, I tell them, "Your story and what you do might not be as dra-matic as that, or it might be more dramatic. You never know. The act itself might not seem like much, but you never know. Stopping to help someone on the freeway or talking to someone, you don't know what kind of day that person was having, and your being there made a big difference in their lives, so how can you make a difference? How can you make a change? I often say, 'The person who is making the change is the person you are looking at in the mirror every morning'." We needed to elect Barak Obama. Today we need to reelect him as he still has many promises to keep. The previous president, George Bush, put us in such a deep hole, it will take five presidents to fully recover.

(top) Border Angels hauling water in the high desert.

(bottom) Migrants in the canyons making use of donations.

Chapter 9

Immigrants and Human Rights

In the end, the struggle for immigration reform is about human rights, the respect for life. Many people besides myself and the Border Angels have been working to educate Americans about the migrant tragedy and its effect on our county's value and the ideas in the U.S. Constitution and the Declaration of Independence. All people deserve respect regardless of their wealth or condition of life. The Border Angels has been devoted to educating North Americans about the need to reform immigration policies and to end the deaths in the desert. After about 25 years of activities, there have been some indications that we are beginning to make a difference.

In the fall of 2009, I was in Guadalajara at a meeting of the Institute of Mexicans Abroad with Isabel Garcia, from Tucson, and others. During the meeting we both got "texted" on our cell phones that Lou Dobbs had been fired from C.N.N. I stopped the meeting, stood up, and announced that to the group. "I've got great news. All these battles that we all fight, we hardly ever see immediate results, but here is a case in point. Lou Dobbs has just been fired." We had been advocating for his removal from C.N.N. for many years and, as I said, had visited the C.N.N. president Jonathan Klein at his headquarters in New York and protested at the C.N.N. headquarters in Atlanta during the first *Marcha Migrante* in 2006. Everybody stood up and chanted, "*Sí se pudo. Sí se pudo*" (Yes, we did it).

That evening in Guadalajara they showed a movie, called "*Los Que Se Quedan*" (Those Left Behind), a very powerful movie about the children and families that get left behind as migrants leave Mexico, Central America, and the Carribean. During the movie I had forgotten to turn off my cell phone, and it rang. It was a bad connection, and I could barely hear. It was Dr. Jose Luis Soberanes, the outgoing president of the National Human Rights Commission of Mexico. He said, "Enrique, this is Dr. Soberanes, and I want to inform you that you have won the National Human Rights Award from the Human Rights Commission of Mexico. Congratulations." I said, "Dr. Soberanes, I am really honored because there are a lot of people who should be getting it before me. I don't think the award should go to only one person. It should be to all of us." He said, "Well, you are the guy we picked." I said, "OK, but I want to dedicate this to Roberto Martinez, my family, and the hundreds, maybe thousands of people who have been involved in this movement, and also I want to dedicate this especially to the migrants." Then he said, "I have to ask you a favor. You can't say anything about it because the new Human Rights president comes in a few days, and he should be the one to announce it." I said OK. This was in November, 2009.

Two weeks later, in December, the new president called and said that they were going to announce it and have a formal ceremony in Mexico City at the presidential palace. I said, "Great, but there's only one thing. I can't go between December sixth and December thirteenth because I have been invited to go to Israel with the Anti-Defamation League. We've been working on this trip for a long time, and the tickets are already pre-paid." A few days later they called back and told me, "We're going to give the award on December 8. The President's calendar is fixed, and we can't change it." I told him that this was really difficult for me because the trip had already gotten security clearance. They had already bought the ticket. They can't change their trip. It's not just me. We discussed it but, of course, I had to go to Mexico.

I went to Mexico City and was allowed to invite a couple of people so I asked my dad and my brother. My dad wasn't feeling very well. He was already 90 years old. But he was feeling better on December seventh, and we flew there. It was top-notch all the way. They picked us up at the airport and took us to a hotel. The next day, they came to pick us up and took us to Los Pinos, the presidential residence. The room was packed. In the front row they had one seat for my dad. But I had to ask for them to let my brother sit by him since he was hard of hearing, and he wasn't feeling well. The ceremony was beautiful. Afterward, they showed a video that they had prepared about our work. First Raul Placencia, the President of the Human Rights Commission, spoke. After the movie, they called me up to the podium, and the President of Mexico, Felipe Calderón, put the gold medal over me, and I got to give a speech. I was very emotional and told them about the migrants. I told them that the future of Mexico was in Mexico, not in the U.S. I told them about how Mexico's own immigration policies need to be changed. Sometimes in the U.S., I get criticized for not talking about Mexico's shortcomings with regard to immigration. But I do when I am in Mexico. When I am in the U.S. I tell the U.S. what I think should be happening here. But I always say the truth. I told them about my dad and how he too was a migrant who came north for economic reasons. He got a visa, something he would not qualify for today. My dad saw to it that all of us got a college education. Most of us have post-graduate degrees. All five of us are bilingual and bicultural. We are all very proud of our Mexican roots and very respectful to the U.S. My dad is my hero. Here is the text of my speech. It summarizes what I have been trying to do for many years.

Mr. President of the Republic, Attorney Felipe Calderón Hinojosa, President of the National Commission on Human Rights, Dr. Raul

Plascencia Villanueva, presidium members, members of the media, friends, family, ladies, and gentlemen. It is a great honor and with great humility that I am with you all.

Today we come to celebrate the work of one person or a small group, but this recognition is not only about an individual or an organization. It is about many thousands of individuals and organizations that make it possible every day to improve the condition of our people. We are all the same race, the human race.

Today's celebration is about our heroes, to whom I dedicate this recognition. It is for the migrants, from Tijuana to Chiapas, who give shelter and love to our children who are walking in the desert; it is for *Grupo Beta* that gives our brothers and sisters water and health when they are lost; this is also about Roberto Martinez (may he rest in peace), who was the pioneer and leader in the movement for human rights at the border; it is about the migrants who are the lifeblood of our movement for justice, who seek only an opportunity to improve their lives, a job, reunification with their families, some bread for their families to eat.

This award is also in recognition of my personal hero, my father, Luis Morones Pelaez, here with us after 90 years of life, a native of this wonderful city of Mexico, son of Luis N. Morones. My father gave us everything and went "north," temporarily, as millions have done, and 55 years later, we continue to live "temporarily," in the "North," but we continue to remember that, thanks to God, as our President said, "We are Mexicans wherever we stand." Born here or there, we are Mexicans, not just Mexicans, but very proud and fortunate to be Mexican, and we never forget this.

My mother, Laura Careaga, is the heart of the family, from the beautiful city of Culiacán, Sinaloa, where my brother, Luis (also with us), was born. Luis is a person who works tirelessly for migrant children who have been separated from their parents' love and support. My sister, Laura, was born in the magnificent city Tijuana, Baja California, and she worked at Father Hidalgo Center in San Diego. My younger siblings, Nora (and her son, Joshua) and Pedro Antonio (and his son Luca) were born in San Diego, California. Thanks to our parents the five of us brothers and sisters are university graduates, bilingual, bicultural, and committed to serve and love, as taught by our Catholic faith. "When I was hungry you gave me food, when I was thirsty, you gave me drink." This is the mission of the Border Angels.

My father taught me that change begins with the person we see in the mirror every day. Change is carried out with actions, not just words, and that we must live the change we want in the world. "Faith without works is dead."

What change? NOT ONE MORE DEATH! REFORM NOW! Today a Oaxacan mother made coffee (American, not Veracruz coffee, which is now too expensive!) for her husband, possibly for the last time, because this morning he went north. He gave his last kiss to his sons and daughters as they slept, so that the next day they will have enough to eat and they do not have to go north. *Mexicanos*, do not go!

What change? NI UNA MUERTE MAS, REFORMA YA! (NOT ONE MORE DEATH! REFORM NOW!) When we, the Border Angels and *Gente Unida,* crossed the country in February, 2006, in the *Marcha Migrante* traveling through 40 cities in 20 states in 27 days, we told people about the reality of the border and asked the people in "the North" to take to the streets to call out for humane immigration reform. Millions took to the streets in that historic spring, in March, April, and May of 2006, and we marched, too.

What change? We are children of the sun, children of the moon, from Aguascalientes to Zacatecas, with Aztec or Zapotec blood. We are Mexicans, and Mexico's future is here in Mexico, not the U.S.. Mexicans, do not go!

Marco Antonio Villaseñor was five years of age, went with his father who was working in the north, but he did not return alive. He died of thirst, cold, in terror along with 18 men, who were killed just because they wanted jobs. Mexican children, do not go!

Lucrecia Domínguez just wanted to join her husband but died in the arms of Jesus, her 15-year-old son, in the desert. His daughter, Nora, wept. Mexican women, do not go!

Our brothers or sisters as unidentified Central Americans are badly treated in their own country and ours. As my friend, Dr. José Luis Soberanes Fernández, says, we cannot ask the north to do what we do not do in the south. Central Americans, do not go!

Luis Ramírez, who came north looking for the "American dream" and instead found the "American nightmare," was brutally beaten by three young racist Americans. He was killed in Shenandoah, Pennsylvania, just for being a Mexican. Mexicans, do not go!

How many more? Many more have been lost in the desert, the mountains, in the river, canals, the car trunks, the murderous smugglers. They have been killed, kidnapped, raped. Mexicans, do not go! Whether 6,000 or 10,000, no one knows the exact number of how many have been killed by the wall of death, the Wall of Shame, the policies of Operation Gatekeeper. Mexicans, do not go!

A few days ago, the world celebrated 20 years since the fall of the Berlin Wall, which killed fewer people in its history than a summer in the desert between Mexico and the U.S.A.! Today, they do not allow families to talk to one another through the fence in Friendship Park, located between San Diego and Tijuana. For decades this was the only place where families could gather on both sides of the wall to share friendship and love! Friendship and love have no boundaries. Friendship Park is the heart and soul of immigration reform. We will reopen Friendship Park! We must build bridges of communication and love and not walls of separation and death.

How can the world celebrate the fall of the Berlin Wall, when we, Mexicans, die due to a wall? We die due to lack of employment. We die because of lack of opportunity. Did my husband arrive in the north safely? My son? My daughter? Or was he swallowed by the road? Thousands are missing. Who are they? Where are they? North America has much to admire, but it is not right that its people demand drugs, and kill our police and our future. They ask for our natural resources and destroy our chance to live in our homes. They ask for workers and do not give us papers. Our brothers and sisters do not have a "legal" way to go north, but they are hungry. Not one more death. REFORM NOW!

Mexicans, do not go. The future of Mexico is in Mexico, not in the North. When I was in professional baseball working with the San Diego Padres, I arranged for them to play in Monterrey, Nuevo León. In August, 1996, we had regular-season games against the New York Mets, and in San Diego and New York the world saw what we know to be true, that there is no other place on earth like Mexico. We love our country.

We are proud of our beloved Mexico. That's what our left-handed pitcher, Fernando, said! We are a country of respect. Benito Juárez told me! We are a country of faith. Saint Juan Diego told me! We are a country of heroes. The *Niños Héroes* told me! We are a country of Champions. Lorena Ochoa told me! We are a country of hope. An indigenous friend told me, Generoso! We are a country of songs. I was told by (Pedro) Infante, Santana, MANA, Lila (Downs), and Julieta! We are a country of joy. Cantinflas told me! We are a country of beauty. Frida told me! We are a country of literature. Octavio Paz told me. We are a country of values. My father Luis told me. We are a country of love. Margarita told me. We are a country with great confidence and a future. My president, Felipe, told me!

A Mexican is a Mexican where he or she stands, and I stand today as ever strongly with my country, Mexico, in my heart, my soul, and my future. When I am traveling or in the field or in the desert . . . I just need to smell the tortilla, hear the mariachi, see the *Tapatío* to be filled with excitement and pride in my precious roots. But better yet, best of all, is to see a father embracing his wife, his son, his daughter, in their home after a long day of work here in Mexico, knowing that we are all safe, knowing that everybody has enough to eat, knowing that we all have freedom, and knowing that we all have a chance here. Mexico is the future.

Again Thanks, Dad. Thanks to everyone here and there, because for me there is no doubt that I live to love my dear Mexico.

After this speech the opportunities for enlarging the Border Angels grew. One of the exciting developments for us has been getting to know the First Lady of Mexico, Margarita Zavala. The first time I met her she was not yet the First Lady. I had been asked to give a talk about immigration at a forum for Mexican presidential candidates in Tijuana. I didn't endorse any of the candidates but had the message that we needed immigration reform in Mexico as much as in the U.S. and that we (Mexicans) should not expect them to do in the north (the U.S.) what we do not do in the south (Mexico). She was waiting with me before the speeches with her little girl. I presented candidate Felipe Calderón with a Border Angels *Marcha Migrante I* shirt, which he put on and wore during his speech. After the talks Calderón said, "Now I want to bring out my wife, Margarita." I was surprised to learn that the woman I was chatting with was his wife.

Many months after this, Margarita Zavala saw the tape of my national human rights award presentations, and she called me at my house. I never pick up my phone but let the answering machine screen my calls. At the end of my message I say *"Viva México."* She laughed in surprise as she left the message. She called twice, and then I called her on her cell phone. She wanted to know when I was coming to Mexico because she wanted to talk to me about the Border Angels. The next week I was in Mexico City and we met. She originally had scheduled a half an hour, but we spoke for three hours. I told her about the many activities of the Border Angels, the *Marcha Migrantes*, the water stations, the relief in the fires, the migrant outreach, the political lobbying. One of the subjects that especially interested her was Friendship Park. I told her how another first lady, Pat Nixon, had inaugurated the park in August of 1971 and how it had been essentially closed off by concerns over border "security." I told her how it was a symbol of the friendship between our countries and how sadly people came from all over California and the Southwest to this park to visit their loved ones, but they can't now because it is essentially closed. I told her, "Maybe you can come to the Mexican side of Friendship Park and you could help fix it up." She agreed and so on January 25, 2010, she came. We met in Tijuana, along with the Governor of Baja California, José Guadalupe Osuna Millán, and then we drove to the park. She fell in love with it and told the Governor that she wanted the Mexican side renovated. A year later she returned to open up the new Mexican park. It looks fantastic, and we are all very grateful.

Since then we have worked to invite the first ladies of both countries, Michelle Obama and Margarita Zavala, to come to Friendship Park for a joint ceremony. Having these two important women there will capture the true spirit of the park: love has no borders. We are working hard on that, along with others on both sides of the border.

Getting the National Human Rights Award opened up lots of doors to get the message out. In 2010, I went to Chiapas, Mexico, three times. We formed an alliance with a shelter for migrants there. We help out by letting people know of their work and helping them get donations. Other similar shelters exist on the northern border.

Enrique Morones with Mexico's then first lady, Margarita Zavala de Hinojosa, Baja California Governor Guadalupe Osuna Millan, and others. Here, Morones petitions for the remodeling of Parque de playas (the Mexican side of Friendship Park), January, 2010.

There are three migrant shelters where we help. In Tijuana there is *La Casa Refugio Elvira* headed by Micaela Saucedo. In Mexicali there's *Hotel Migrante* run by a group called *Angeles Sin Fronteras*. The third one is *Casa Bienestar Jesús Cristo* in Tapachula, Chiapas. The one in Chiapas works mainly with Central American migrants who have lost their limbs and other tragedies on the trains when they were crossing into Mexico.

Here, in San Diego, we have lots of dedicated volunteers. The person who has been instrumental in organizing them is Pam Calore. We finally have an office after 25 years, located in Sherman Heights, where people can drop off items to be donated to migrants. There, we have meetings and we have people who have taken leadership roles, like Raul Hernandez, who does the website designs; Mar Caredenas, who does the listserve; and Pamela Calore, who is also a photographer and artist. We have students, like Sophia, who is administering the Home Depot Program. We have a young girl, Keren, and her sister from City College, who are starting campus support groups. We have Pepe Villarino and other musicians. We have a lot of volunteers who make up the organization.

With the volunteers, the Home Depot program is probably the biggest thing we've done in the last five years. We go there almost every week. We have an adopt-a-Home Depot program with a model here in San Diego, and we hope to have it spread across the country. What we do is that we have people who live near a Home Depot keep an eye on it. Once a month they go to that Home Depot and see if there are any problems, such as migrants being harassed by Minutemen. If there are problems, they let us know, and we will know what to do. This program has really grown. We have the one near the Qualcomm Stadium, which is our home base. We go not only to give the workers sandwiches, water, and the like, but also to give them know-your-rights cards. Some men might say, "We worked for a week and didn't get paid," in which case we would turn them over to the worker's-rights center. A lot of it is networking and being a conduit. Maybe we are not the ones to handle the problem, but we can put them in touch with people who can. For asylum cases we can turn them over to *Casa Cornelia* with Carmen Chavez. The Home Depot Program is key to us because when migrants come to the U.S. to work lots of them go there. We have student groups that come from all over the country and want to meet immigrants, so we go to the Home Depots. There are about 25 in all of San Diego County, and we cover lots of them.

In the past few years we have had new opportunities to work with others and reach out to talk about human rights and the borders. In Oaxaca in southern Mexico, in particular, we are expanding to work with establishing micro-loan programs to help build small businesses.

The last two years, working with the groups who are with the workers living in the canyons in northern San Diego County, we had a 5-K Walk for Workers. This money is being used to give loans to small businesses in southern Mexico so that they do not have to come north to survive. People can start their own businesses, breadmaking, carpentry, sewing, and the like. It's a very powerful idea, and we want to develop this. These things will take time.

Regarding the politics of immigration reform, getting the award has also helped with visibility for the human-rights agenda on the national and state levels. I have had the opportunity to travel to Washington, D.C., several times to consult on policies, and we have been very active in California state politics. I am setting up meetings with the Hispanic Caucuses both in Sacramento and Washington, D.C. We want to pass the Dream Act. There are a lot of little victories, such as defeating anti-immigrant bills in Arizona. These are steps in the right direction. I think we are going to have a Dream Act and that President Obama will sign an executive order to stop the deportations, and that is going to happen in the next few years. I think that we will have immigration reform but not until the first two years of President Obama's second term.

The struggle for the human rights of immigrants goes on. In 2011, major-league baseball gave a civil-rights award to Carlos Santana, Ernie Banks, and Hank Aaron. Carlos Santana took the microphone and live, before a huge audience at Turner Field in Atlanta, right before the Braves played, he said, "Georgia and Arizona should be ashamed of themselves because of the racist legislation they have passed." Some people cheered, some people booed, but he had the courage to say it. Georgia had recently passed an Arziona-like law. Later at the press conference he elaborated, saying people ought to boycott Georgia and Arizona. This gave us a boost in morale, when a figure of the stature of Carlos Santana comes out opposed to racist immigration laws. Even though we have had some setbacks legislatively, we will get reform bills passed.

We will continue with our work: the *Marchas Migrantes*, the water stations, the Home Depot programs, speaking out against racism, spiritual tributes, and dedications. Gradually, because of the "Power of One," the unseen effects of the work of hundreds of individuals, awareness about the human rights and the plight of the immigrant is growing. But people continue to die along the U.S.-Mexican border, and this is a constant reminder of our failure to live up to the promise of our country. We continue to have an urgent mission to keep on working for those who lack a voice.

Suggested Readings

T.C. Boyle. *The Tortilla Curtain.* New York: Viking, 1995.

Daniel G. Groody. *Border of Death, Valley of Life: An Immigrant Journey of Heart and Spirit.* New York: Rowman & Littlefield Publishers, 2007.

Paul Hoffman, ed. *Front Line USA: Threats, Attacks, Arrests and Harrassment of Human Rights Defenders.* Dublin, Ireland: Front Line, 2004.

Sonia Nazario. *Enrique's Journey: The Story of a Boy's Dangerous Odyssey to Reunite with his Mother.* New York: Random House, 2007.

Joseph Nevins. *Dying to Live: A Story of U.S. Immigration in an Age of Global Apartheid.* San Francisco: City Lights Books, Open Media, 2008.

Jorge Ramos. *Dying to Cross: The Worst Immigrant Tragedy in American History.* New York: Harper Collins, 2005.

Luis Alberto Urrea. *The Devil's Highway: A True Story.* New York: Little, Brown and Company, 2004.

Appendix A
Juana's Letter

Mr. Enrique Morones,

It is with much grief that I have received your kind letter. I still cannot accept the reality of the death of my beloved son, Marcelino Martín. What can I say about my son? That he was a noble, hard-working, honest young man who wanted to get ahead and to get to know a country so many young people dream about, in spite of my premonition as a mother. Even before he left, I knew something serious would happen to him. I asked him, begged him with tears in my eyes, not to go. Here in Mexico he probably would not lack for anything. He was working and, with God's help, he was getting ahead. He did not listen to me. Later, my anguish grew when no one could tell me his whereabouts. My relatives living in the United States were waiting for him but he had not arrived, had not even called. Later, I learned my premonition had come true. His death has invaded me, and left me with so much anguish and pain in my heart and my soul; nothing has been able to lift it. He was only beginning to date a girl and had not yet married. At 19, as they say, he had barely begun to live. So much is heard and seen on television about the dangers of trying to cross the border to the neighboring country, but this does not deter people. They risk it thinking it's not going to happen to them. I don't know how he died, if in the desert or the river. However it was, it is irreversible and tragic. Since he left home, my anguish barely lets me sleep at night, and I haven't stopped crying. The neighbors who knew of my sorrow would encourage me by saying bad news travels faster than good news, and so it was until I received his body and gave him a Christian burial surrounded by the large number of people who accompanied us on that last good-bye. May God give us the strength to give him up, because my resistance continues to make me suffer.

May the Lord and the Holy Virgin repay you for your worthy efforts to ease the pain of so many families who have lost their loved ones. There is no doubt that a human being must suffer in order to understand our terrible ordeal.

Thank you so much for your kind, gracious letter.

Juana

Translated by Vivian Otero Barrera
Published in *Latino Studies*, 7.4 (Winter 2009): 515-16.

Appendix B

Partial List of Immigrant Deaths 1994 to 2007
(And a notes on the deaths of a sample of migrants)

CALIFORNIA ·· Víctor Nicolás Sánchez · Adolfo Pérez Hernández · Daniel Barrientos · Santos Orozco Aguilar · Raúl Hernández Soria · Sandra Edna Durán · Jesús Medina Contreras · Edgar Venegas Brambila · José Gutiérrez · Melquiades Gómez Baca · Martha Rivera García · Benito González Cruz · Benito González Serrano · Javier Rojas Bracamonte · Juan José Romo Zetina · José Luis Garza · Roberto Acegueda López · Román Robles Rojas · Reynaldo González Corona · Juan Lara Mentado · José Santos López Fonseca · Luis Ramírez Escobar · Felipe Aragón Anzaldo · Salvador Sánchez Sánchez · Reyes Jiménez Zamora · Javier Zatarain Gamboa · José Guadalupe Martínez · Celerino Alvarado · Benito Pacheco López · Marcelino Ramírez · Lorenzo Gaytán Ramírez · Cipriano Orozco · Pedro Calixto Maganda López · Eliseo Santos Carmona · José Luis Centeno · Zenaido García de los Santos · José Manuel de la Luna · Martín Leonardo Hernández · Modesta López · Olivia Cruz Juárez · Carlos Béjar Vázquez · Alejandro Cornejo Reséndiz · Felipe de los Santos · Enedina Beatriz Enciso Palma · Juan Guillén Domínguez · Benito Ávalos Romero · Juan Carlos Córdova · Sergio Jiménez Villanueva · Antonio Zacarías González · Gregorio Ortiz · Pedro Morales Ramírez · Félix Zavala Ramírez · José Manuel Moreno · Guillermo Ayala Méndez · Daniel Loera Salinas · Carlos Loera Salinas · Gustavo Barajas · Oscar Alcalá Gopar · Práxedis Salinas Palma · Juan Pablo Córdova · Ramiro Castorena Martínez· Álvaro Padilla Herrera · Virginia Murillo Díaz · Nicolás Méndez · Alfonso Villalobos Rodríguez · Gustavo Bañuelos · Onésimo Ledezma Hernández · Enrique López Maciel · Héctor Daniel Torres · Luis Oswaldo García Bando · Raúl Castro Ortiz · Abraham Tomás Cortés · Roberto Valdez Valencia · Roberto González · Rafael Valenzuela Zúñiga · Teresa Urbano García · Lorenzo Barrera Cortez · Benjamín Zaragoza Arias · Jorge Ramírez Amarillas · Pablo Meraz Rosales · Eloise Maya Rodríguez · Roberto Vázquez · Joel Godoy Juárez · José Herrera Martínez · Juan José Pérez González · Raúl Santana Nájera · Raúl Anzures Galarza · Osvelia Tepek · Trinidad Santiago Martínez · Catalina Enríquez Néstor · Gustavo Muñoz Cázares · Gerardo Gaspar Chompa · Alejandro Ramos Zavala · Juan Magaña Hernández · Emigdio Vera Pérez · José González Chacoya · Alejandro Mendoza Pacheco · Rosario Torres Pérez · Osvaldo Serrano Reyes · Enrique Santos Nieto · Aristeo López García · Isaías López Alvarado · Joaquín Mendoza Chávez · Francisco Ramón Segura Saldaña · Alfonso Guillén Guillén · Ismael García Vásquez · Herminio Martínez Altamirano · Alfredo Barriga Ruiz · Roberto Sánchez · Mario Alfredo

Clemente Díaz · Antonio Rocha Trejo · Rafael Arias Sotero · Agustín Chaparro Huitrón · Héctor Jesús Méndez Brown · Verónica Manzanares Cárdenas · Fredi Barrera Sánchez · Pastor Raya Zamora · Yuridia Rodríguez Sánchez · José Luis Rey Lugo Vidal · José Froylán Morales Camacho · Gregorio López Otero · Daniel Martínez Osvaldo · Isabel Gabiño Díaz · Gil Aroche Ayala · Armando Gilberto Quiroz Jiménez · Guillermo Rodríguez Barajas · Fernando González Gallegos · Rodolfo García Campuzano · Rafael Espinoza Espinoza · Guadalupe Romero González · Ramón Arenas Olmedo · José Alfredo Godoy Chávez · María González Flores · Ana Gabriela González López · Víctor Manuel Ramírez Ochoa · Jorge Chaparro Garduño · César Pineda Vizcaíno · Clara Zaldívar García · Juan Ochoa Valencia · Germán Santos Cruz · Maximino Rojas Cordero · Valentín Monge Cárdenas · María Torres Contreras · José Carmen Herrera Orea · Domingo Estrada Pérez · Roberto Ramírez González · Pablo Ramírez González · Marco Antonio Bustamante · Apolinaria Santiago Hernández · Evedo Osorio López · Guillermo Osorio López · Gerardo Escobar Luévano · Juan Manuel Rodríguez Vásquez · Rodolfo Gómez López · Oswaldo Zamorano González · Juan Carlos Purata Purata · Gil Félix Medina · Serafín Andrade · José Carmen Raya Hernández · Remigio Salomón Barrientos · Bertha Carrillo Topete · José Ramírez Tirado · Cruz Piña Reyes · Noé Beltrán Mendoza · Ulises Ortiz Cruz · Florencio Mendoza Luciano · Roberto Xoyatla Orzuna · Arturo Mercado Arriaga · Victorino López Santiago · Moisés Díaz García · Mario Carrillo Ruiz · Juan Gabriel Gregorio Granados · Cristina González Ramírez · Pedro Ismael Orozco Gómez · Adán Mosqueda García · Emeterio Castañeda Aguirre · José Espinoza · Longinos Benítez Barrera · Raúl González Cruz · Julio Manuel Flores Salazar · Margarita Campos Romero · Roberto Bailón Camacho · Bellanira Ramos González · Juan Domínguez Morales · Guadalupe Ramírez · Francisco Morales Olvera · Francisco Paredes · Miguel Angel García Navarrete · María del Carmen Dorantes Durán · Marcelino Valdivia Montes · Raúl Mendoza Díaz · Manuel Carrillo Rivera · Osvaldo González Guzmán · José Refugio Valle Gamiño · Roberto Saavedra Carrazco · Daniel Hernández González · Aureliano Cabrera Morales · Justino Rugerio Rodríguez · Felipe López Rodríguez · Antonio Morales Morales · Irma Estrada Gutiérrez · Wilfrido Santiago Alvarado · Fernando Salguero Lachino · Noel Guzmán González · Julio César Gallegos Durán · Evaristo Carrasco Luna · Eduardo Díaz Hernández · Cayetano Robles de la Torre · Luis Illescas González · William Benítez Cervera · Guillermo Cedillo Balderas · Margarita Melchor Rangel · Natalio Teodoro Solís · Pedro Felipe Juárez · Luis Manuel Ramírez Melgoza · Raúl Figueroa Cortés · Marcos Sánchez Sarabia · Adán Figueroa Ortiz · Homero Meza Fernández · Alvaro Rueda Hernández · Antonio Rentería Martínez · Oscar Cardoso Varón ·

Uriel Asunción Hernández · Celia Flora González Reyes · Víctor Aguilar Fernández · Efraín Barragán · Oscar Abel Córdova Vélez · Leonel Huicaza Valenzuela · Antonio Galván Carrillo · Fernando Mejía Alamilla · Epifanio Cárdenas Silva · Adrián Rogel Jaime · Olegario Márquez Morales · Isidro Zavala Lerma · Jesús Zavala Lerma · Andrés Valerde Hernández · José González Betan · Abel Uribe Mercado · Edithtrudis Agatón Flores · Juan Eduardo Chávez Campos · Jesús Nolasco García · Ambrosio Ramírez Olivera · Carlos Segura Rosales · Jorge Alvarado Hernández · Felipe de Jesús Cervantes Hernández · Joel León Montenegro · Armando Hernández López · Jaime Suárez Cázares · Daniel Toro López · José Angel Leobardo Márquez García · Gonzalo Cardeña Solorza · Andrés Artemio Ríos Canseco · Filemón Bañuelos Herrera · José Ricardo Ríos Aguilar · Alejandro Rodríguez Cazorla · Samuel Yépez Cervantes · Martín Mendoza Blaz · Rogelio Rodríguez Cobarrubias · Javier Martínez Fuentes · Antonio Ventura Torres · José René Benítez Tadillo · Jaime Rocha Franco · Sebastián Díaz Avila · Juan Martín Picasso Vega · José Ricardo Ríos Aguilar · Jaime Martínez Martínez · Pedro Pérez Pedroza · Moisés Pérez Pedroza · Amado Morales Herrera · José Luciano Pérez Madrid · Rodrigo Olmos Esparza · Ildegardo Esteban Miranda · Oscar Vicencio Reyes · Irineo Aguilar Soto · Everardo García Estrada · José García Proaño · Alfredo Rodríguez Ramos · María del Socorro Duarte Negrete · Enrique Luna Alaniz · Miguel Angel Pérez Salazar · Timoteo Roblero Morales · José Jiménez Toala · Fabián Gutiérrez Rico · Oliver Mosqueda del Castillo · Mauricio Gutiérrez Lozano · Julio Millán Avila · Loreto González Molina · Adelaida Hernández Luna · Arturo Magallón Galarza · María Félix Tepal González · Silvia Barrera Tapia · Romualdo López Fuentes · Teresa Inés Vera Navarrete · María Cruz Rosas · Marlene Tapia Gutiérrez · Evaristo González Mendoza · José Jorge Rivera Zúñiga · Ana María Padilla Echeverría · Miguel Zaragoza Santiago · Juan Manuel Rodríguez Ramírez · Leticia Hernández Sánchez · Ismael Apolinar · Osvaldo Martínez García · Iraida Medina Aguirre · Margarita Villa Rodríguez · Raymundo Sánchez Gómez · Onésimo García Ramírez · Melitón Juárez Cruz · Noé Juárez Cruz · Rubén Barragán Larios · Jesús Manuel González Aguilera · Sergio Figueroa Ceja · Javier López · Gustavo Uribe Durón · David Hernández Zúñiga · José Encarnación García Valle · Pablo Alberto Alvarez García · Carlos Adrián Corona Jiménez · Pedro López López · Luis Alejandro Bautista · Guadalupe Zacarías Hernández · Héctor Manuel Osaki Carreras · Hugo Serrano Angeles · Mario Orozco Zurita · Macario Vázquez Zurita · Manuel Moranchel Quintero · Roberto Montiel · Serafín Rivera López · Marcelo Figueroa Vázquez · Cupertino Retama Solís · Fernando Dimas Bernal · Margarita Jarquín Pérez · Jorge Lemus Contreras · Emeterio Flores Sotelo · Inocente Bueno Eriza · José Ediberto Rodríguez Ruiz · Gerardo

Torres Ramírez · Arcadio Rodríguez Pérez · Guillermo Valdovinos García · Rafael Silva Romero · Arturo Suástegui Altamirano · Juan Luis Romero Garnica · Alejandro Jiménez Ruiz · Luis Ortiz Murillo · José Manuel López Guzmán · Felipe de Jesús Díaz · José Antonio Flores Pérez · Belzar Haro Rodríguez · José Julián Gómez Ponce · Roberto Avila Rodríguez · José Luis Urióstegui · Roberto García Hernández · Miguel Estanislao Vicente · Antonio Gutiérrez Sánchez · José Arnulfo Estrada Pérez · Antonio Figueroa Velásquez · Nicolás Pablo Sánchez Martínez · Nemesio Castañeda Vargas · Manuel López Sánchez · Gabriel Vargas Méndez · José González de Santos · José Roberto Haros Avitia · Trinidad Orozco Hernández · Marcelino Diego Castro · Jesús Plascencia Peinado · Leonardo Plascencia Morales · Roberto Castell Guzmán · Manuel Hernández Solís · Jorge García Rivera · Jorge Lua Landín · Efigenia Chávez Solorio · José Antonio Araujo Alvarez · Efrén Ruiz Reynoso · Enrique Belman Díaz · Carmen Albarrán Romero · Irma Castillo Hernández · José Trinidad Ruiz Lozano · Fidel Ramírez López · Vicente Coto Muñoz · Rubén Mendoza Sánchez · Horacio García Vásquez · María Mota López · Alma Rosa Pérez García · Amelia Calvo Asunción · Luisa Olivera Santos · Gerardo Martínez Castro · José Luis Pantoja Arteaga · Feliciano Canseco Aguilar · Luis Morales Acosta · Jesús Herrera Romero · Prócoro Monterrosas Serrano · José Arturo Gutiérrez Salinas · Arturo Domínguez Moreno · Plutarco Ambriz Ambriz · Efraín Morales Cervantes · Raúl Hernández Echeverría · Aarón Vega Cruz · Johnathan Zaldívar Mimila · Juana Francisca Castellanos García · Miguel Castellanos García · Salvador Castellanos García · Juan Marcial Albino · Agustín Romero Luna · Jesús Márquez Pacheco · Santos Velásquez Villegas · Héctor Rubén Moreno Valle · Antonio Ramírez Vargas · José Trinidad Hernández Atilano · Salvador Gerardo Sánchez Hernández · Maricarmen Risas Ponce · Luis Campa Molina · Cliserio Cristóbal Castañeda · Bernardino Valdez Huendo · Raúl Alfonso Campos Favila · Héctor Uriza Garzón · Margarita Hernández Rodríguez · Roberto González Pantoja · Nilson López Vallinas · Luis Manuel Aguilar García · Leticia Torres Solís · Hugo Barajas Pérez · Bertha de la Merced Tapia · Cristina Castro Lucas · Arnulfo Flores Badillo · Edgar Adrián Martínez · Mario Castillo Fernández · Julián Ambros Málaga · Enrique Landero García · Reyno Bartolo Fernández · Raymundo Barreda Maruri · Raymundo Barreda Landa · Alejandro Marín Caludio · Lorenzo Hernández Ortiz · Heriberto Badillo Tapia · Sergio Ruiz Marín · Marina Juárez Herrera · Efraín González Manzano · Jesús Ulloa González · Irene Islas Morales · Alberto Vigueras Alejandre · Luis Urzua Delgadillo · Anselmo Catalán Nava · Carlota de la Cruz Flores · Sergio Hernández Jiménez · Wilfrido Valdez San Agustín · Agustín Torres García · Javier Hernández Hernández · Rosa Espino Jacobo · Arturo López Cevallos · Heraclio de

Jesús Morales · Pedro Zaya Vergara · Miguel Angel García Torres · Humberto Díaz Hernández · Ignacio de Loya Carmona Carmona · José René Labastida Cortez · Natalia Pérez Hernández · Víctor Ever Murillo Arzate · Margarita Miranda Martínez · Manuel de Jesús Espinoza Gallegos · Rogelio Meléndez Sánchez · Marcelino González Aquino · María del Carmen León Camacho · Salvador Botello Cortés · María Isabel Pacheco Madera · Quirino Lara Primo · Gonzalo Mora Carrillo · Socorro Arroyo Hernández · David Barrios Pérez · Samuel Núñez Cruz · Refugio Belisario Jiménez · David de Jesús Flores Villarreal · Esteban Eleazar Alcántara · Alberto Aparicio Hernández · Arturo Arriaga Villa · Luz María Centeno Zárate · Humberto Abad Carpio · Alejandro Acuña Isaías · Oseas Díaz Montejo · Austreberto Pérez López · Zacarías Hernández Díaz · Esperanza Vallejo Hernández · Rafael Carrillo Méndez · Sósimo Miguel Rodríguez · Juan Antonio Gómez Díaz · José Carmen Pamatz Molinero · Luis Ernesto Gil Cota · Julio César Hernández Morales · José Luis Vásquez Gutiérrez · Joel Aguilar Pérez · Ramón Díaz García · Raúl Lule Hernández · Daniel Castro Bayón · Rogelio Contreras Navarrete · Gustavo Chávez Muñoz · Rubén Salcido Mesa · José I. Márquez Cervantes · Marcelino Luna Cabrales · María Pinita Ramírez Marques · Luis Francisco Hernández López · Martín Gómez Horte · José Antonio Alcaraz · David Girón López · Rubén Pérez Sánchez · Guadalupe Fragoso Dávalos · Manuel López López · Cresencio García Estrada · Néstor García Aburto · José Luis Pérez Cruz · Romualdo Quintero Gutiérrez · Adolfo Ríos López · Justino Hernández Barrios · Pedro Jiménez Briones · Jorge A. Salas García · Cristóforo Meza García · Orlando Eric Altamirano Jiménez · Martín Aguilar Meza · Zeferino Pérez Padilla· Florina Pérez Padilla · Martha Olivia Cevallos García · Ismael Bravo Vargas · Alejandro Gomes Farías · Ana María Vargas Mendoza · Isaac González Cevallos · Juan Hernández Gamino · Victoria Sánchez Gasca · Elvia Rumbo Leyva · Moisés Fitz Flores · Esteban Nieto Caballo · Rodolfo Jáuregui Quiñónez · Mario Alberto Bastidas Jiménez · Juval Martínez Jiménez · Juan José Escalera Valdez · Juan Santiago Ocampo · Claudia Morales Salinas · Juan Carlos Quero Quero · Marcos César Moreno Solano · Arturo Martínez Olmos · Edgar Valdez García · Paulino Solís Verduzco · Eduardo Díaz Estrada · Gildardo Díaz Guerra · Luis Alonso Ceja González · Juventino Bravo Curiel · Jesús Eduardo Cervantes Camacho · Mario Ortega Pérez · Leonardo Sánchez Plácido · Severiano Miguel López · Gustavo Sánchez Delgado · Javier Margarito Cortez · Gerardo Bailón Martínez · Eréndira Jiménez García · Santos Jiménez Pagle · Alma Rosa Cárdenas Moreno · José Luis Baltasar Santiago · Leónides Ortega Melo · J. Guadalupe Damián Govea · Esteban Vargas Lemos · Salomón Vega Guerrero · Maribel Solís Blas · Juan Piña Soto · Julio César Villegas Gómez · Ana María Morales · Verónica García Alvarez · Fernando López Coria ·

Francisco Gómez Anaya · Héctor Chavarín Zárate · Adriana Patricia Zavala Negrete · Raúl Sánchez Chávez · Rosa Lilia Parada Bermúdez · Juan Armando de León Pérez · Jaime Zúñiga Barragán · Reynaldo Valenzuela Camacho · José Refugio Ortega Nieves · Rosalba Maldonado Romero · Carlos Echeverría Bribiezca · Iván Escalante Maldonado · Rufino Cordero Castillo · Martín Vilchis Angeles · Francisco Juárez Ozuna · Gabriel Alvaro López Herrera · Pedro Ramírez · Marcos Gildardo Montes · Rosa Valencia Torres · Rafael Mata García · Jesús Sáenz Mendoza · Felipe M. Ramírez · José Jesús Santana · María del Consuelo Morales Avalos · Luisa Zagal García · Lorena García Temozihui · Estanislao Torres Coria · Emilio Ramírez Morato · María Oralia Varela Padilla · Pedro Contreras González · Noé Carreón Rojas · Gustavo Vallejo Delgadillo · Elvia Huerta Gocobachi · José Luis Nicolás González · Miguel Angel Duarte Meza · Víctor Arzola Méndez · Raúl Garibay Alvarado · Gabriel Mercado Cota · Víctor Carrillo Medina · Tomasa Ochoa Zamora · José Antonio Bautista Herrera · Bernardino López Gabriel · María del Carmen Rodríguez Martínez · María del Pilar González Hernández · Gumercindo Reyes Loxada Hipal · Onésimo Salazar Cruz · Manuel Pérez Chávez · Eliseo Benítez Santos · Rubén Salcido Meza · José I. Márquez Cervantes · Dionisio Alvarado Gutiérrez · Alejandro Gómez Farías · José Guadalupe Carcamo Ortigoza · Felipe de Jesús Aviña Jiménez · Carlos Manuel Rivera Chávez · Leandro Leyva Luna · Miguel Mejía Amarillas · Miguel Castro Rodríguez · María Oralia Varela Padilla · María Isabel de la Cruz Medina · Rubén Vargas Bernal · Erick José Antonio Noriega Patiño · Iván Fontes López · Alvino López Bautista · Angélica Echiveste Limón · Gerardo Rodríguez Zaranda · Alejandra García Alvarez · Víctor Mondragón de Jesús · Aurelio Ramírez Barraza ·· ARIZONA · Juan Ezequiel Gutiérrez Andrade · Evelio López Laines · Rosa Palomino Pérez · Raúl Mendoza · Everardo Amaya Jiménez · Ana Claudia Villa Herrera · Miguel Angel Vázquez Godínez · Elidia Martínez Macario · Rolando Morales Solano · Arturo Acosta Soto · José Martín Molina Pánuco · Efraín Molina Ruiz · Abel Acero Díaz · Jorge Ayala Trujillo · Francisco Hernández Morales · Roberto Plascencia González · Pedro Velázquez Quintero · Telésforo Franco Hernández · César Ramos Fernández · Héctor Carrizosa López · Juan Mejía Alvarez · Martín Ortega Campos · Marco Antonio Cortez Iriqui · Marco Antonio Castillo Puga · José Ramón González Salazar · Cuauhtémoc Lavín Valentín · Héctor Lavín Martínez · Martín Martínez Zaragoza · Roberto Ramírez Ramírez · José Guadalupe Llanitos Villalobos · Manuel de Jesús Flores Artalejo · José Antonio Rodríguez Hernández · Aarón Moisés Delgado López · Alejandro Félix Barraza · Carmen Margarita Rodríguez Martínez · Guillermo Barrera · Ana María Pacheco Mejía · Manuel de Jesús García Coronado · Gerardo García Cota · Teófilo Camacho Salinas · José Macías Fernández · Verónica

Nadia López Muñoz · María Eugenia Aguillón Díaz · Olivio Velázquez Pérez · Modesto Santos Flores · Francisco Chima Mil · Cirilo Larios Guzmán · Ramón Figueroa Chávez · Abelino Armenta Martínez · Antelma Graciela Castelán Gutiérrez · Cándido Rodríguez Pacheco · Roberto Baltazar de Jesús Zamora · María del Rocío Bravo Candia · Nátali Hipólito Enríquez · Luis Roberto Morales Avendaño · Emma Monteclaro Castillo · Rodolfo Lagunes Beltrones · Rafael Ortega Ramírez · Jesús Vidal Ramírez · María Inés González Alvarez · Jesús Magaña Otero · Alfredo Ubieta Domínguez · José Inés Díaz González · Delia Moreno Pérez · Gerardo Nevares Gallegos · Carlos Miguel González Corona · Edmundo Angel Selvas Ruiz · Zenón Reséndiz Nieto · Teresa Cabrera Baltasar · Herlindo Martínez de Jesús · Eusebio García Pérez · Julio Alfredo Lagunas Castillo · Enrique Soto Pacheco · Juana Medina Butanda · Marina Montaño Mercado · Héctor Guadalupe Sánchez Murrieta · José César Mendoza Mendoza · Fermín Aguilar Rabadán · Maura Zacarías Sánchez · María Cruz Ruiz · Yolanda González Galindo · Juan Manuel Acosta Rojas · Alberto Márquez Castelán · Víctor Talavera Figueroa · María E. Morales Sierra · Jesús Rodríguez Coronel · Omar Sánchez Guevara · Justino Vidal Bautista · Janet Mata Méndez · Juan Manuel Ruiz Dávalos · Gerardo Rosas Martínez · José Luis Vergara Flores · Juan Rodríguez Sánchez · Víctor H. Dávila Ehuan · José Carlos Wicab Chable · Adán Martínez Faustino · Salvador Mendoza Guízar · Abel Martínez Faustino · Hugo Sánchez Acevedo · Manuel Gómez Hernández · Oscar Cervantes Melquíades · Froylán Flores Hernández · José Guadalupe Rico Sánchez · Ramón Gámez Mesa · Guillermina Herrera Guzmán · Enedina Torralba Martínez · Laura Vargas Ortiz · Pedro Basulto Neri · Antonia Méndez Méndez · Eutiquio Dorantes Marín · Modesta Pacheco Pérez · Mario Calderón Jiménez · Roberto Arturo Olvera Morales · Julio Yáñez Hernández · Rosalía Bazán Miranda · Juan José Ontiveros Lizárraga · Raúl López Sánchez · Demetrio Vélez García · Cázares Sánchez · Miguel Angel Chigüil Arres · Paula Isela Romero Palacios · Yolanda Novoa Ponce de León · Isaura Viviana Medina Paredes · Pedro Mejía Palacios · Leticia Herrera Navarro · Angel González Hernández · Elizabeth Esther Gómez Balbuena · Luis Cáseres Cabrera · Juan Pedro Patiño Rojas · Felipe Sánchez Nájera · Fernando Mendoza Cruz · Alicia Adela Sotelo Mendoza · María del Rosario González Ortiz · Víctor Juárez González · Sergio Pérez Pescador · Abelardo Pérez Hernández · Armando Rosales Pacheco · Buenaventura Ayala Zamora · Iván Centeno González · Tiburcio Agudo Martínez · Adela Salas Pérez · Guadalupe Nieto Octaviano · Lauro Barrios Domínguez · María Dolores Espinoza · Rosario Sánchez Roguel · Roberto Bautista López · Anastasio López Guerrero · Martín Espinoza Cruz · José Aldegundo Romero · Enrique Mendoza Castillo · Jorge Alonso Mireles · Andrea Alcántar

Cruz · Alvaro Segovia García · Alberto Maldonado Viveros · Irasema Martínez Jiménez · Carlos Armando Gracián Bustamante · Petra Verónica Tenerio Soto · Juana Martínez Sánchez · Abel González Domínguez · Esteban Durán Aburto · Hermila Romero Carreño · Jorge Montes Montejano · Marco Antonio Grado Miramontes · Dalvin Eugenio Urbina Krik · Santiago Pacheco Ramírez · Didier García Villanueva · Lidia Dimas Téllez · Catalina Ventura Mendoza · Irene González Hernández · Elizabeth Juárez Río Frío · Graciela Hernández Alvarado · Lorena Chávez Martínez · Prócoro Flores Ortiz · Heriberto Núñez Robles · José Angel García · Ernesto Alonso Gutiérrez Ramírez · Casimiro Chavira Ramos · Héctor Salcedo Hernández · Gerardo Rubén Jiménez Martínez · Gerardo Román Jiménez Martínez · Carmelo Monárrez Ramírez · Diego Enríquez Quevedo · María Dolores Martínez Vega · Samuel Fernando Arce Muñiz · Wenceslao Torres Torres · Rafael Alberto Palma Salas · Tomás Molina Pérez · Mario Bustillos Sallet · Cástulo Salazar Ontiveros · Carlos García Aguirre · Miguel Fructuoso Hernández · Martín Grijalva Martínez · Miguel Ochoa González · Arturo Heras Espinoza · Esteban Bulmaro Olvera Alabarrán · Jesús Rojas Villa · David González Soriano · Víctor Acevedo Díaz · Alonso Hernández Hernández · Claudio Martínez Cortez · René Rodríguez Ramírez · Francisco Trujillo Ruiz · Simeón Díaz Cruz · Miguel Ochoa González · Domitila Mondragón Alvarado · Rogelio Cruz Cervantes · Jaime Rodríguez Gutiérrez · Sofía Rubio Chávez · Paula Hernández Tapia · María Guillermina Sánchez Salto · Raúl López de Anda · Arturo Gómez Castro · Antonio Vargas Torres · José M. Raygoza Gil · Alex Sosa Coba · Margarito Escorcia Franco · Arturo Jiménez Gutiérrez · María E. López Gómez · Santiago Arcos Mota · Adilene López Moreno · Rafael López Méndez · Eva Hernández Escárcega · Norma Rodríguez Amado · Margarita Ríos Rodríguez · Eraís Quintana Martínez · Florencio Pedroza Guadarrama · Angeles Contreras González · Víctor Galindo Torres · Ricardo Pantaleón Santiago · Felipe Hernández · Gonzalo González Saldaña · María Luisa Lozano de la Rosa · Martín Moreno Montero · Beatriz Cuautle Gutiérrez · Alfonso Caloca Vargas · Juana González Ramírez · José Lara Avila · René Reséndiz Rodríguez · Santos Fabián González Paredes · Blanca Estela García Reyes · Ramiro García Abarca · Mauro Santos Tolentino · Rogelio Sánchez Santoyo · María de Jesús Candelario Rodríguez · José Luis Hernández Aguirre · Rubén González Miranda · José Salazar Velarde · Cristina Domínguez Librado · Alejandro Hernández Badillo · Jesús Torres Santiago · Máximo Barrera Esquivel · Domingo López · Lucía Agustina López · Leonel Tuxpan Jarno · Raúl Estrada Frías · Joel Hernández Aguila · Eledi Sánchez Cirilo · Manuel Escandón Morales · Ismael Tepox Gamboa · Dolores Trejo Ramírez · María Dolores Trejo · Alberico Córdova Robledo · Oscar Irineo Santillán · María de Jesús Ruiz García · Francisco Cueva Ochoa ·

Zenaida Colmenero Dircio · María Mancero Rojas · Jesús Beltrán Hernández · Dámaso Rosales Zamudio · Emma Mercedes Quintal Parra · Elizabeth Hahuatzi Martínez · Maribel Muñoz Bustos · Roberto Rodríguez · Maricarmen Xaltenco Serapio · Alejandrina de la Soledad Félix Sánchez · Leandro Bautista Alba · Juana Santacruz García · José Alfonso Abortes · Eugenio Reyes González · Alfredo Escobar López · Alma Delia Cruz López · Pablo Espinoza Hernández · Cecilio Cabrera Pedro · María de la Luz Magaña · Alfredo Campos Márquez · Oscar Borbón Mendoza · José Antonio Pérez Rubio · Jorge Cruz Becerril · Liliana Robles Enríquez · Carmen A. Robles Enríquez · Lorna Robles Enríquez · Gonzalo Gómez Gómez · Cesario Ruiz Cortez · Albino Montes Campos · Amalia Ortiz Licona · Celso Villa México · Antonio Mora Martínez · Mariano Durán Saucedo · María Dolores Vera Mendoza · Gabriel Torres Alcalá · Palemón González Avilés · Efraín Salinas Zagal · Noé Alvarez López · María del Carmen Infante Hernández · José Andrés Aguayo Contreras · José Luis Rodríguez Tavares · Francisco Chávez Mújica · Josefina Martínez Sánchez · José Refugio Ferral del Angel · Rocael Hernández Gómez · Martín Gallegos Pérez · Guillermo Federico Sánchez Lomelí · Juan Matías García Zavaleta · Roberto Torres Ramírez · Teresa Vela Velásquez · Azucena Ortiz · Miguel Angel Rodríguez Ortiz · Miguel Angel Rodríguez Esparza · Federico Medina Rodríguez · Avelino Andrés Cabrera González · Genaro Rosales Martínez · René Olvera Medina · Elías Hernández Hernández · Mario González Hernández · Herminia Fuentes Sánchez · Luis Fernando Noriega Ayala · María Cristina Hernández Pérez · Sergio Enrique Mejía Pérez · Manuel Hernández Martínez · Jorge Aburto Zamorano · Juan Tovar Hernández · José Angel López Cárdenas · Zita Islas Uribe · Adriana Aparicio Ortega · Eliseo Vargas Luna · Adrián Díaz Dionisio · Honorio Ramírez Martínez · Armando Valadez · Antonio Alvarez Solórzano · Keila Velásquez González · Pedro Xichicale Tlapalcoyoa · Antonio Aguirre Bustamante · Leticia Villagrán Flores · Javier Gabriel Valdez · María Alejandra Orea Guzmán · Juan Manuel C. Mojuto · María Teresita Galván Avila · Nora Cecilia Huertas Hernández · Rocío Quintero Ramírez · Teodomiro Vázquez Marcos · Efrén Gutiérrez Hernández · Juan Miguel Cano Elvira · Carlos Valentín Bahena · Patricia Cortázar Espitia · Guadalupe Cayetano Cornelio · Antonio Rolon Hernández · Angela Contreras Rojas · María Guadalupe Vázquez Saavedra · Fortino Vázquez García · Elonina López Alfaro · Saúl Domínguez Luján · Héctor Romero Correa · Delia Herrera Atilano · Sergio Benítez Hernández · Sergio García González · Ricardo Olivares Martínez · Juan Carlos López Hernández · Marcial Pérez Alvarez · Mauricio Sasas Guerra · Agustín Hernández Jiménez · Amado de Jesús de Jesús · Abigail Dalia Rodríguez López · Martín de Jesús Bernabé · Irene Ayllón Velásquez · Miguel Rodríguez

Marentes · Ernesto Rivelino Ramírez Blancas · Flora María Reyes Cruz · Zenaida González Robledo · Alfredo Fabián Gudiño Ruiz · Juan Miguel Velásquez Navarro · Manuel de Jesús Sánchez Rodríguez · José Fernando Martín Fuentes · Víctor Manuel Plascencia Basilio · Hilda Roblero Roblero · Nicolás de Jesús García Ventura · José Manuel Gómez Cruz · Alma Rosa de la Torre Hurtado · Juan Antonio Nila Valdivia · Pascual Carbajal Maya · Florencio García · Lorenzo López Díaz · Lucio Hernández Hernández · Carlos Ramón Bejarano Cañez · Miguel Díaz García · Efraín Castro Ramírez · Jaime Monroy Gamiño · Miguel Angel Laurel · Antonio Gómez García · Rubén García Gamiño · Ana Cruz García · Juan Carlos Rico Orihuela · Rosa María Arriaga Castillo · Rafael Martínez Ruiz · Nahum Martínez Solano · Juan Mendoza · Martín Chaires Corral · Magdalena Antonio Pérez · Jorge Rolando Cano Yeh · José Antonio Ruiz Campos · Atanasio Castañeda Ramos · Miguel Angel Velázquez Hernández · Abel Alemán Cabrera · Daniel Haro Martínez · Faustino Bermeo Rayón · Agustín Rita Santos · Nicolás Padilla Reyes · Isidro Gutiérrez Reyes · Ciro Vega Velásquez · Pedro Zárraga Ramos · Hilda Hernández Baltasar · Carlos Francisco Casanova Estrada · Oscar Antonio Arrequidez Ortega · Adrián Garnica Hernández · José María Martínez Espinoza · Adelfo Rosales González · Leopoldo Alvarado Sánchez · Oscar Chávez Torres · Florencio Monroy Rocha · Sotero Gómez Viveros · María Lucía Martínez · Daniel Alvarado Patiño · Carlos Castro Ilescas · Antonio Avila Cortés · Margarito Aguillares Hernández · Gabriel Ortega Flores · Raúl Ramos Chávez · José Paz Arriaga Mercado · María del Carmen Sabino García · Concepción Anfreas García · Rolando Pérez Vázquez · Juan Leonel Lizárraga · Jaime González Pablo · Fortino Soto Armenta · Rosario Muñoz Berelleza · Francisco Javier Acosta Sandoval · Reynael Cortínez Roblero · Rodrigo Miranda Rivera · Feliciana Tadeo Hernández · Reyes Salazar Campos · Tomás Soto Granados · Norma Alicia Moreno Hernández · Fidelina Bravo de Marzán · Yecxal Alvarado Monterrosa · Mario Alberto Rodríguez Pérez · Alvaro Ramos de Castilla · Altagracia Marbella Tapia Guillén · José Juan Pacheco Salazar · Aurelio Torres Soto · Carmen Avila Vargas · Juan Manuel Guerrero Díaz · Federico Campos Mayor · Armando Antúnez Mendoza · Socorro Ayala Beltrán · Sofía Beltrán Galicia · María Cristina Salinas Gonzales · María Fabiola Palomares Ríos · Mario Soto Trejo · Carlos Alberto Argueta Lezama · Emilio León Domínguez · Raymundo Santana Hernández · Armida Martínez Preciado · Roberto Parra Orduño · Marcelo Infante Pereira · Leopoldo Méndez Murrieta · Rosa Viviana Torres Corona · Emelia Pérez Santiago · Edgar Isidro Díaz Estrada · Issac Melo Mejía · Adalberto Tello Encarnación · Isaías Espinoza Gonzales · Olivo Martínez de la Cruz · Manuel Luis Ramírez Herrera · Teófilo López Manrique · Jovita Martínez Agudo · Angel Alberto Lizárraga · Silvia Rodríguez Gómez ·

Víctor Machuca Quesnell · César Andrés Moya Vargas · Blanca Estela Ferreyra Vidal · Maricruz Frías Amador · Ismael Gómez Herrera · Raquel Hernández Cruz · Ana Montes Gámez · Oscar Valderrábano Hidago · Librado Tolentino Velazco · María de la Cruz Flores Martínez · Nancy Navarrete Hernández · Marcos de la Cruz Sandoval · Julio César Romero Espargo · Paulina Morales Exiquio (María Adriana Alvarado Leyva) · Josefina Useda Barajas · Mario Alberto Díaz Ponce · Sergio Cabrera Hernández · Reyna Figueroa Espinoza · Omar Francisco Ortiz Camacho · Luciano Limón Sánchez · Verónica Dueñas Ramírez · Jesús Hernández López · Rogelio Juárez Torres · Eufracia Cuautláhuatl Cuautle · Rafael López Méndez · Erais Quintana Martínez · Florencia Pedroza Guadarrama · José Martín Alcaraz · Gonzalo González Saldaña · Santos Fabián González Paredes · Ramiro García Abarca · María de Jesús Candelario Rodríguez · José Luis Hernández Aguirre · Domingo López López · Saúl Segura Oliveros · Alonso Caloca Vargas · Salvador Macedo de la Paz · Eleuterio Guzmán Hernández · Alfredo Rosas Ramos · Isidro Domínguez Ledesma · Miriam Maldonado Peraza (Medrano Pedraza) · José Angel Miranda Escobar · Pablo Gerardo Lázaro · Enrique Vital Aguinaga · Francisco Javier Sánchez Aguilar · José Enrique de Jesús Serrano · Eduardo Amador Munguía de la Cruz · Albertano Herrera Liborio · Aurelio Ríos Venegas · Antonia de la Cruz Andrade · Karina Portillo Cortez · Madilio Luis Gutiérrez Pérez · José Luis Pérez · Manuel Batalla González · Rosa Peña Ocampo · Jesús Román García · Gustavo Adolfo González Cruz · José Alfredo García Martínez · Aurora Cuambo Magallón · Enrique Morales Flores · Isaías Juan Gálvez Pérez · Telésforo Arroyo Santos · Leonardo Plata Escamilla · José Trinidad Alcocer Martínez · Leticia Ruiz Ruiz · Dante Roldán Flores · Abel Salinas Cortes · Humberto Hernández · José Narciso Hernández · Oscar Francisco León García · Edith Cuevas Avelar ·· NEW MEXICO ·· Víctor de Jesús Montalvo · Eunice Avila Hernández · Remedios Rojas Fernández · María Montellano Jiménez ·· TEXAS ·· Espiridión Rosales · Alberto Salazar Martínez · Juan Espinoza · René Ortiz · Ofelio Linares · Francisco Chávez Hernández · José Antonio Larrazola · Apolonio Ramírez · Pablo Vilchis Bravo · Luis Alejandro Lejona Barrón · Benjamín Cabrera Velásquez · Telésforo Velásquez · Mario Valdez · Alfredo Izaguirre · Menor Torres · Sixta Cruz Cruz · Miguel Saldívar Medrano · Marco Antonio Hernández Reyes · Cleto Ramírez Vite · Andrea Cortez · Luis Villanueva González · Juan Pablo González Amaya · Gerardo Muñiz · José Israel Rodríguez Lara · Amador Pasillas · Sergio Vargas Calderón · Hugo Vargas Calderón · Arturo Cardona Omaya · Javier Cárdenas Hernández · Christian Escamilla Noriega · Roberto Ramírez Cubos · Rufino Lara Guevara · Rafael Mejorada Castillo · Jorge Carlos Luna Muñoz · Valentín Caballero Landeros · Rogelio Nolasco Márquez · Javier García Herrera · Miguel

Ramírez Vázquez · Jesús Pérez Luna · César Arenas · Osiel Valdez González · Alejandro Hernández García · Javier Estrada Soto · Aquiles Peña Chávez · César Campos Gómez · Humberto Martínez Galindo · Ramón García Jiménez · Nemesio Vallejos · Froilán Cervantes Muñiz · Jesús Manuel Marentes Escobar · Juan Manuel Marentes Escobar · Antonio Sánchez Morales · Pedro Solorio Enríquez · Hiram Martínez Mendoza · Juana Avila Martínez · Salvador Colín · Eliud Cardiel Rodríguez · Manuel López · Antonio Espinoza Luna · Salvador Martínez Martínez · Ricardo Salazar Juárez · Sergio Rodríguez Almaguer · José Luis Huizache Ramos · Armando Martínez Alvarado · Adrián Flores Hernández · Carlos Villalobos Sandoval · Filiberto Carrillo Ramírez · José Alonso Figueroa de la Luz · Bernardo Carbajal Pineda · Alejandro García Gasca · Gerardo González de la Rosa · Héctor de Jesús Hernández Hernández · Bernardo Carbajal Pineda · Daniel Rojas Lara · Alejandro Torres Ramírez · Enrique Miranda Colín · José de Jesús Gómez Regalado · David Serrato Mondragón · Martín Dorantes Castillo · Josué Escobar Castillo · Ricardo Ortega Díaz · Juan León · Juan Manuel Flores García · José Fidencio Sierra Maldonado · Iván Arellano Zavaleta · Alicia Ponce Juárez · Gustavo Chagoya Estrada · Raúl Salas Longoria · Osvael Samayoa Calderón · Juan Hernández Hernández · Juan de la Cruz Aranda Rodríguez · Rosina Loma Ramírez · Fidel Martínez Mojica · Roberto Pérez Gaytán · Marcelo Ortiz Maldonado · Juan Fidel Segovia Martínez · Gustavo Oropeza Carrasco · Antonio Loredo Flores · Armando Pío Acosta · Joel Andrés Rivera · Rogelio Castro González · Javier Aguilar de Dios · Juan Fuentes Bernos · Julio Arturo Verástegui Martínez · José Tomás Medrano Martínez · Roberto Pozos Onofre · Magdaleno Ramírez García · Raúl Martínez Delgado · Jesús Martínez Prado · José Isabel Rodríguez Martínez · Juan Valles Romero · Juan Manuel Cervantes Arriaga · Carlos Rayas Rodríguez · Alvaro Salinas Salinas · César Gutiérrez Hernández · José Carrizales Méndez · Martín de la Garza Cruz · Manuel Mendoza Ledesma · Miguel Angel Martínez Castillo · Enrique Bustamante Córdova · Yolanda Hernández Morales · Jerónimo Mendoza Guzmán · Raúl Albarrán Ortiz · Alberto Arévalo Gutiérrez · Jorge Cabrera Tovar · Vicente López Barbosa · Pablo Salazar Puente · Eustorgio Fermín Flores Martínez · Joaquín Contreras Rabino · Leobardo Ortiz Pérez · Enrique Guzmán Jiménez · Roberto Zavala Alvarez · René García Pérez · Isaac Hernández · Rubén Alonso Segura · Fernando Fraga Ortega · Jorge Alberto Reyes · Hermilo Olvera Patlán · Luis Antonio Gallardo Mendoza · Marcos Pacas Gutiérrez · Esperanza Flores de Almanza · Nelson Herrera Refinos · José Eduardo Arriaga Alonso · Esthela Ruiz Torres · José Víctor Jiménez Torres · Jorge Garcés Rogel · Emilio Maqueda Villeda · Juan Carlos Juárez Castillo · María del Carmen Martínez · José Manuel Ayala Flores · José Montero Gómez · Alfonso

Villalobos Alvez · Francisco Bazares · Jaime Montoya Ramírez · Edgar Villalbo Salgado · Miguel Angel Martínez Herrera · Juan Antonio Sixto Contreras · Jorge Murillo Ríos · Gustavo García Rosales · Gildardo Sánchez · Luisa Hernández Cruz · José Vélez Leos · Luis Augusto Juárez Castellano · Guillermo Castilla Islas · Romualdo Martínez Estévez · Eduardo Rea Ramírez · Eugenio Saucedo Valdez · Adolfo Sánchez Salgado · Marcial Rodríguez Niño · Enrique Mancera Ortiz · Ramiro Ramírez Martínez · Eutimio García Ibarra · Leonarda Rodríguez Castillo · Gustavo Miranda Granados · Guillermo Solís Ramírez · Norma Ramos Becerra · Félix García Domínguez · Andrés García Esquivel · Juan Maldonado Silva · Sergio Alberto Llanas López · Joel Hernández Domínguez · Edgar Hernández Sánchez · Rubén Pérez Ríos · José Sánchez González · Arturo Villaseñor Vega · Agustín Vega Bastida · Verónica Ramírez Ramírez · Mateo Ledezma González · Jesús Trujillo Vallejo · Miguel Palafox Carreón · Salvador Dávalos Rico · Magdalena Luna Ulloa · José Juan Prieto Soto · Roberto Vargas Domínguez · Heriberto Parra Estopellano · Rosendo Eduardo Luna Domínguez · José del Carmen Rivero · María Inocencia Velásquez Fernández · Antonio García López · Osvaldo García Herrera · Eric Rojas Márquez · Raimundo González Rangel · Juan Martín Alvarado Pérez · Avelino Reyes Promotor · Manuel Idanguray Puente · Juan Villanueva Martínez · Sergio Armando Salinas Cisneros · Rubén Alanís · Lenin Guzmán Cuevas · Abraham González López · Guillermo Luna Rivera · Raúl Quintos Cuéllar · Humberto Espinoza Gallegos · Ernesto Zúñiga · Teresa Delgado Mercado · Juan Carlos Cuenca Valadés · Teresa Villa Dimas · Salvador Flores Torres · José Quintero Vargas · José Cruz Quintero Vargas · José Jesús Quintero Vargas · Francisco Espinoza Vázquez · Miguel Angel Rivera Castillo · José Narmo Ramírez Mendoza · Florentino Mayerido Rico · José de Jesús Andrade Lugo · Esaúl Balderas Quiñónez · Tereso Delgado · Eusebio de Haro Espinosa · Dionisio Muñoz Pérez · Marcelino García Colunga · Manuel Romero Torres · Ricardo López Puente · Marcial González Padrón · Teodolfo Rubio García · Francisco Javier Copián Rangel · Alfonso Rodríguez Rodríguez · José Gregorio Méndez · Antonio González Reina · Daniel Castillo Morales · Ricardo Morales Barajas · Alfredo Garza García · Eleuterio Arteaga · Ricardo García Márquez · Armando Maldonado · Walter María Sandoval · José Antonio Ramírez Martínez · Luis Hernández Guerrero · José Francisco Cabello Pichardo · Miguel Hernández Ibarra · Juan José Domínguez Paredes · Gustavo Cruz · Octavio Vargas Jaimes · María Elena Gutiérrez · Martha Llanas Torres · Santos Espinoza González · Juan Alberto Treviño Baez · Humberto Frabe · José Vargas · Guillermo Zamora Acosta · Hugo Antonio Solís Cruz · Rubicel Solís Cruz · Concepción Prieto Bermea · Celestino Ledesma · Martha Irma Cervantes Juárez · Ismael Cerda Hernández ·

Ambrosia González Hernández · Fortunata Hernández Rebollar · Feliciano Flores Hernández · Enrique García Sosa · David Benítez González · Fernando Arellano Covarrubias · María del Refugio Hernández Rojas · Juan Narciso Muñoz Ruiz · Emmanuel Godínez Muñoz · Martha Herrera Buendía · Santos Peña Lara · Rubén Mejía Cruz · Casimiro Morales Temich · Ebodio Martínez Muñoz · Jaime Alvarado Salazar · Geisel Rodríguez García · Heriberto Mendoza Faz · María Antonia Zamudio Martínez · Tranquilino Ramírez Sotelo · Fidel González San Juan · Pascual Ramírez Huerta · Efrén Gómez Morales · Rogelio Vargas Almaguer · Juan Escalante Torres · Carlos Gutiérrez Alvarez · Juan Francisco González Martínez · Fernando Martínez Gallardo · Pedro Enrique Martínez Flamenco · Ariel Linares Cruz · Agustín Meléndez Soto · Isabel Aguillón Mejía · Hugo Ventura Mejía · Mario Ramírez Luna · Gustavo Martínez Loredo · Filiberto Cruz Ferrer · Pedro Hernández Mata · Víctor Pérez Hernández · Efraín Olguín Cabrera · Eusebio Herrera Avila · Gabriel Salazar Rangel · Juan Antonio Sánchez Reyes · Salvador Zapata Castillo · María de Jesús Pérez Olvera · Fernando Camarena Reyes · Juan Jesús Quevedo González · Daniela Navarrete Rivera · Agustín Quintanilla Tamayo · César Martínez Briones · Manuel Hernández Rodríguez · Juan Campa Ortiz · Teresa Santos Baena · Ronulfo Salazar Martínez · Felipe Trejo García · Oscar Guadalupe García Mata · María Luisa Navarro Romero · Angélica Gómez Martínez · Platón Mar García · Oliverio Aguilar Ramos · Andrés Roberto Barrón García · Alfonso Yáñez García · Roberto Rodríguez González · Douglas Arturo Flores Martínez · Jorge Robledo Martínez · Luis Manuel Galeno Vásquez · Cirino Ramírez Otero · Maribel García Solano · Eleazar Ramírez Peña · José Alberto Cabrera Gómez · Ismael Carrizales Espinoza · Maximino Rubio Romero · Erick Iván Salas Reyes · Alberto García Vásquez · Leopoldo Celso Lucio Camargo · Andrés Salas · Asunción Sánchez Espinoza · Alma Delia Simón Fernández · Armando Hernández Silva · Rubén Zurita Bengas · Camilo Aguilar López · Angélica García Morena · Antonio Vaca · Jaime Espinoza Torres · Cristóbal Díaz Castillo · Marco Antonio Ponce Piniero · José Guadalupe Macuil Zamora · Noé Tapia Colorado · Ernesto Alonso Martínez Ibarra · Maximino Ramírez Hernández · Rafael Puerta Romero · Ricardo Hernández Cruz · José Guadalupe Carrión López · Isaac Ortiz Bello · Víctor Manuel Aragón López · Antonio Vences Morales · Angélica Ramírez Canchola · José Dolores Camacho García · Pablo Morales Martínez · José Cano Carranco · Enrique Navarrete Merlos · Francisca Zárate Pérez · Arturo Barbosa Medina · Pablo García López · Enriqueta Noria Huerta · Rogelio Corrales Muñoz · Javier Alfonso Cepeda Gallegos · Francisco Torres Santiago · Vicente Ramón Moreno · Amado Franco Vidales · José Carlos Demes Contreras · Melitón Yáñez Hernández · Rosalba Martínez · Francisco Huerta

Medina · Antonio Solano Chávez · Antonio Vázquez Avalos · Juan Carlos Morán · Víctor Manuel Saavedra · Ezequiel Gutiérrez Hernández · Ernesto Gómez · Oscar López Aregil · Juan Antonio Díaz Rivera · Domingo Crispín Gapi · María Antonia Trujillo · Ramón Herrera Núñez · Arturo Blancarte González · Matías Acosta Hernández · Juan Hernández Cisneros · Jusafat Rivera Miranda · Martín Daniel Vargas · Elías Salaiz · Celso Leyva Montalvo · Juan Miguel Núñez Cabada · Bernarda Torres Macedo · Luis Palma Guerrero · Horacio Alejandro Sandoval · Carlos Lázaro Díaz Díaz · Rutilio Salinas Aragón · Jesús de Jesús Menchaca Martínez · Gonzalo López Castañeda · Israel López López · José de Jesús Menchaca Martínez · Gonzalo López Castañeda · Raúl Pérez Mora · Florentino Villa Medellín · José Guerra Ledesma · Job Martínez Cobos · Antonio Rico Medina · José Inez Guel Vásquez · Roberto Gasca Mancera · Florencio Antonio Gámez Gutiérrez · Saúl Flores Manzano · Rigoberto López Hernández · Alejandro Martínez Banda · Orlando Losada Molina · Salvador Ramírez Barrón · Juan Gabriel González Ortiz · María Mata Montiel · Alfredo Huerta Ruiz · Cecilia Martínez Pizarro · Mario A. Montellano Jiménez · Alicia Rentería Bautista · Faustino Aguirre Palma · Evaristo Narváez Cantú · Santiago Martines Medina · Pedro Pérez Escobar · Ernesto Baltasar Sánchez · Salvador Rodríguez Palacios · Amalia Martínez Esparza · Germán Rivera Negrete · Anastasio Bolaños Ordóñez · José Luis Torres Reza · Rafael Ruiz Hernández · Máximo Reséndiz García · Carlos Sánchez Perdomo · Ezequiel Arceo Guerrero · Israel Molina Fuentes · Guadalupe Barrientos Padrón · Jesús Sánchez López · Antonia León Zavala · Alejandro Sánchez Santos · José Correa Aguado · Pablo Segura Salinas · Alberto García García · José Luis Pérez Reyes · José Manuel Espino · Víctor A. Márquez Salas · María Rosa Guerra Sánchez · Evelio Castro Loredo · Gloria Sonora Morán · José García Ledesma · Darío Vera Martínez · Alfredo Alfaro Gutiérrez · Amado Zúñiga Díaz · Antonio Santos Ventura · Jesús Anaya Pastor · Saúl Garza Pedroza · José L. Medina Cobarruvias · Faustino Olvera Rodríguez · Luis López Arellano · Antonio Edmundo Hernández Serrano · Pánfilo Santiago Martínez · Julián Landero Ruiz · Angélico Pérez Vásquez · Rosa Pérez Guzmán · José Mauricio Pérez Guzmán · Angel Gabriel Pineda de la Cruz · Roberto Reyes Luna · Jesús Villa Ramírez · Galdino Morales Hernández · Francisco Mata Arias · Serafín Rivera Gámez · José Luis Ramírez Bravo · Elisendo Cabañas González · Roberto Rivera Gámez · Edgar Gabriel Hernández Zúñiga · Marco Antonio Villaseñor Acuña · José Antonio Villaseñor León · Juan Carlos Castillo Loredo · Ricardo González Mata · Oscar González Guerrero · Juan José Morales · Juan Carlos Estrada Alvarez · Juan Carlos Franco Romero · Héctor Ramírez Robles · Mateo Salgado López · David Bernabé Pérez González · Eliseo Carrillo Hidalgo · Pedro Chávez · Eduardo · Ismael González Mejía ·

Regino Hernández Martínez · Gerardo Dolores Paulín · Jesús Vázquez Barrera · Manuel Herrera Martínez · Alejandro Herrera Martínez · Leopoldo Romero Mandrujano · Rogelio Domínguez Benítez · Cheve Benítez Jaramillo · Catarino González Merino · Ismael Ruiz Castillo · Manuel López Sotelo · Edgardo Tavera Nava · Miguel Angel Nuncio Urbina · María del Carmen Martínez Mendoza · Francisco Javier Aguilar Galarza · Alfonso Puentes Villegas · Mundo Salomón Zanaca · Antonio Salazar (José Antonio Pérez García) · Jorge Luis Meléndrez Ruiz · Issac Ariza Ruiz · Mario Jiménez Terrazas · Marisol López Echeverría · José Armando González Cervantes · Guadalupe Martínez Martínez · David Rama Rez Mendoza · Néstor Salazar Yépez · José Martín Martínez Campos · Damián Serrato Jiménez · Eladio Hernández García · Miguel Sánchez Olvera · Ricardo Rosas Alvarez · Augusta Porfirio Arredondo Luna · Edgardo Ayala Dávila · Ramón Miranda Segovia · Guadalupe César Pérez · José Alfredo Castro Villa · Antonio Hernández Lazos · Abelardo Flores Olascuja · José de Jesús Bañuelos García · Eva Ponce Ramírez · Luis Fidencio Hinojosa Arredondo · José Manuel Gutiérrez Rodríguez · Gerardo Cobillos Ramos · Silverio Cruz Alvarado · Guadalupe Ortiz · Celestino López Espino · Juan Manuel Sandoval Vargas · Rodolfo Guerrero Ruiz · Freddy de Jesús Aban Cano · María Cristina Jiménez Ponce · Pedro García Hernández · Adán López Núñez · Ernesto Aarón Rosas Sánchez · Gabriel Martínez Maya · Felipe Escobedo Gines · José Luis Alejandro Méndez · Florencio Herrera Arteaga · Liberato Aban Cano · Jesús Martínez Antunes · Rosa Isela González Garibay · Huber León Muñoz · Benita Alvarado Venegas · Catalina Juárez Pozos · José Luis Jaime Patiño · Marco Antonio Camacho Rosas · Hermilo Mayen Luna · Luis Javier González Padilla · Melitón Barrera Reséndez · Mónica Martínez Mundo (Garduño Martínez) · María Elena Martínez del Castillo · Guadalupe Balero Gardea · Gerardo Miguel Velasco Martínez · José Socorro Pineda Morales · Roberto Acosta Rodríguez · Esau Gamaliel Pérez Pérez · Miguel Angel Sandoval Mercado · Julio César Lazcano Luna · Gabriel Delgado Parga · Ricardo Martínez Carrillo · Delfino Humberto Sifuentes Favela · José Ventura López · Refugio Desiderio Esquivel · Gabriela Cornejo · Juana Mojica Martínez · Miguel René Morales · Eduardo Sánchez Rodríguez · Ezequiel Martínez López · Antonio Maqueda Sánchez · Guillermo Guerrero Rincón Gallardo · Araceli Rodríguez Zamora · José Luis de Jesús Olivares · Juan G. Cerna Mejía · Enrique Salazar Romero · Gustavo Salazar Romero · Pablo Simón Nicolás · Miguel Torres Ascensión · Luis Enrique Rodríguez Vicencio · Leticia Almazán Carmona · Maricela Pérez Valente · María Esther Segura Juárez · Antonio Millán Mena · René Torres Salazar · Daniel Vázquez Gutiérrez · Miguel Galicia Salinas · Antonio López Ortiz · María de los Angeles Guerrero Rojas · Abraham Loera Alcalá · María

Cruz Mata Montiel · Cecilia Martínez Pizano · Santiago Martínez Medina · Anastacio Bolaños Ordóñez · José A. Hernández Hernández · Salvador Romero Ledesma · Guillermo Murillo Barragán · Gumaro Sánchez Maqueda · María Beatriz Rodríguez Camacho · Paola Juanita Aboytes Guerrero · José Luis Hernández Rodríguez · José Jiménez Sánchez · Fernando Valdez Sánchez · Alejandro Pérez Contreras · Juan Pablo Miranda García · Juan Humberto Ramos Estrada · Alberto Esquivel Grimaldo... and about one thousand migrants not identified...

Appendix C

Myths and Realities about Undocumented Immigrants
(taken from the Border Angels site: http://www.borderangels.org/)

1. **Immigrants don't want to learn English.**
    The development of English proficiency among non-English speaking immigrants today mirrors that of nineteenth- and early twentieth-century immigration when masses of Italian, German, and eastern European immigrants came to America. While first-generation, non-English-speaking immigrants predictably have lower rates of English proficiency than native speakers, 91% of second-generation immigrants are fluent or near fluent English speakers. By the third generation, 97% speak English fluently or near fluently (Shirin Hakimzadeh and D'Vera Cohn, "English Usage Among Hispanics in the United States," Pew Hispanic Forum, Dec. 6, 2007. http://pewhispanic.org/reports/report.php?ReportID=82; Janet Murguia and Cecilia Muñoz, "From Immigrant to Citizen," *The American Prospect,* Oct. 23, 2005, http://www.prospect.org/cs/articles?articleId=10487).

2. **Immigrants don't pay taxes.**
    Undocumented immigrants pay taxes. Between one-half and three-quarters of undocumented immigrants pay state and federal taxes. They also contribute to Medicare and provide as much as 7 billion dollars a year to the Social Security fund. Further still, undocumented workers pay sales taxes where applicable and property taxes—directly if they own and indirectly if they rent (Immigration Policy Center, "Undocumented Immigrants as Taxpayers," November 2007, http://www.ailf.org/ipc/factchecks/UndocumentedasTaxpayer.pdf; Eduardo Porter," Illegal Immigrants are Bolstering Social Security with Billions," New York Times, April, 2005 http://www.nytimes.com/2005/04/05/business/05immigration.html?ex=1270353600&en=78c87ac4641dc383&ei=5090&partner=kmarx).

3. **Immigrants increase the crime rate.**
    Recent research has shown that immigrant communities do not increase the crime rate and that immigrants commit fewer crimes than native-born Americans. While the undocumented immigrant population doubled from 1994 to 2005, violent

crimes dropped by 34% and property crimes decreased by 32%. Furthermore, Harvard sociologist Robert Sampson has found that first-generation immigrants are 45% less likely to commit violent crimes than Americanized, third-generation immigrants (Immigration Policy Center, "Immigrants and Crime: Are They Connected," December, 2007, http://www.ailf.org/ipc/factchecks/CrimeFactCheck10-16-07.pdf; Robert Sampson, "Open Doors Don't Invite Criminals," *The New York Times*, March 11, 2006, A15; Executive Office of the President: Council of Economic Advisors, "Immigration's Economic Impact," June 20, 2007, http://www.whitehouse.gov/cea/cea_immigration_062007.html).

4. **Immigrants take jobs away from Americans.**
   A recent study produced by the Pew Hispanic Center reveals that "Rapid increases in the foreign-born population at the state level are not associated with negative effects on the employment of native-born workers." In fact, given that the number of native-born low-wage earners is falling nationally, immigrants are playing an important role in offsetting that decline. The Urban Institute reports that between 2000 and 2005 the total number of low-wage workers declined by approximately 1.8 million while the number of unskilled immigrant workers increased by 620,000, thus offsetting the total decline by about a third (The Urban Institute, "Trends in the Low-Wage Immigrant Labor Force, 2000-2005," March, 2007, http://www.urban.org/publications/411426.html; Rakesh Kochhar, "Growth in the Foreign Born Workforce and Employment of the Native Born," Pew Hispanic Center, August 10, 2006, http://pewhispanic.org/reports/report.php?ReportID=69).

5. **Immigrants are a drain on the United States economy.**
   The immigrant community is not a drain on the U.S. economy but, in fact, proves to be a net benefit. Research reported by both the CATO Institute and the President's Council of Economic Advisors reveals that the average immigrant pays a net 80,000 dollars more in taxes than they collect in government services. For immigrants with college degrees, the net fiscal return is $198,000. Furthermore, The American Farm Bureau asserts that, without guest workers, the U.S. economy would lose as much as $9 billion a year in agricultural production and 20%

of current production would go overseas (CATO Institute, *CA-TO Handbook for Congress: Policy Recommendations for the 108th Congress*, http://www.cato.org/pubs/handbook/hb108/hb108-63.pdf; Executive Office of the President: Council of Economic Advisors, "Immigration's Economic Impact," June 20, 2007, http://www.whitehouse.gov/cea/cea_immigration_062007.html; Derrick Z. Jackson, "Undocumented Workers Contribute Plenty," *The Boston Globe*, April 12, 2006, http://www.boston.com/news/globe/editorial_opinion/oped/articles/2006/04/12/undocumented_workers_contribute_plenty/).

6. **Undocumented immigrants are a burden on the healthcare system.**
    Federal, state, and local governments spend approximately 1.1 billion dollars annually on healthcare costs for undocumented immigrants, ages 18-64, or approximately $11 in taxes for each U.S. household. This compares to 88 billion dollars spent on all healthcare for non-elderly adults in the U.S. in 2000. Foreign-born individuals tend to use fewer healthcare services because they are relatively healthier than their native-born counterparts. For example, in Los Angeles County, "total medical spending on undocumented immigrants was $887 million in 2000—6 % of total costs, although undocumented immigrants comprise 12 % of the region's residents" (Source: The Rand Corporation, "RAND Study Shows Relatively Little Public Money Spent Providing Healthcare to Undocumented Immigrants," November 14, 2006, http://www.rand.org/news/press.06/11.14.html; Dana P. Goldman, James P. Smith, and Neeraj Sood, "Immigrants and the Cost of Medical Care," *Health Affairs* 25, no. 6 (2006): 1700-1711).

Appendix D
31 Silent Epitaphs

Rosa Mercedes Domínguez Cano. 30 years old from Yucatán. Died in the desert of Arizona in 2002.

Reyno Bartolo Hernández from Veracruz, a small business owner 37 years of age. Died of dehydration outside Yuma.

Raymundo Barreda Maruri, 54 years old. Died in the desert by the side of his 14-year-old son, Raymundo junior. Wanted to make money to fix up his house.

Elisendo Cabanas Gonzales, 27 years old from Puebla. Suffocated to death with 18 other people in the back of a trailer truck in Texas.

Delia Herrera Atilano, 45 years old. Died of dehydration in the desert while her 15-year-old daughter searched for water. Was trying to join her husband in Ohio.

Carlos García Bravo, 18 years old from Guanajuato. Died in the desert outside Tucson.

José Guadalupe Juárez López, 40 years old. Shot by a *coyote* outside Red Rock, Arizona.

José A . Pérez Rubio, 16 years old. Died of a heart attack while under the watch of Border Patrol. Had some candy and a phone number in his pocket.

Pedro Bautista. Died in the womb as his mother tried to cross the desert.

María Dolores Vera Mendoza, 27 years old. Died of dehydration outside Yuma.

Teresa Vela Velásquez, 16 years old from Aguascalientes. Died close to the border along with her brother.

Ricardo Olivarez Martínez, 22 from Sonora. Died while in the hands of Border Patrol.

María de los Ángeles Contreras Rojas, 18 years old from Hidalgo. Identified by her husband Simón.

Floria María Reyes Cruz, 17 years old from Oaxaca. Hit by a car trying to escape Border Patrol.

José Manuel Gómez Cruz, 16 years old from Guanajuato. Crossed with seven other people; died with six of them in the desert due to dehydration.

Víctor Nicolás Sánchez, 30 years old from Oaxaca. Drowned in the Tijuana River.

María Guadalupe Gómez, 37 years old. Died crossing the Río Grande, along with her 16-year-old daughter.

Adriana Martínez Gómez, 16 years old. Died crossing the Río Grande, along with her mother.

Carmen Bustamante Aguirre, 33 years old. Drowned in the Río Grande at dawn in September of 2004.

Jorge Reyes, 26 years old from Mexico City. Looking for work to support his wife and new baby. Died of Dehydration in South Texas.

Ramiro Martínez, 48 years old from Michoacán. Had crossed multiple times in between harvest seasons. Died with fellow workers.

Martha Torres, 30 years old from Jalisco. Planned to get a housekeeping job in California. Died of suffocation in the back of a truck.

Angélica Moreno, 12 years old from Chihuahua. Died traveling with her mother and brother in southern California.

Humberto Gallegos, 32 years old from Durango. Had been a farmer but couldn't make enough money to live on. Died in the Sonoran desert.

Rosa González Garibay, 23 years old from Sinaloa. Died along with her unborn child south of Tucson.

Marco Hernández Reyes, 18 years old. A musician from Tamaulipas. Died crossing into Texas with childhood friends hoping for work.

Hermilo Patlán, 37. Died in the desert outside Calexico. Needed work to help finance his mother's medical bills.

Edgar Salgado, 42 years old, father of five. Died on his second trip into the States, after being deported from California.

María Guerrero, 19 years old from Veracruz. Was trying to join her fiancé in Texas. Drowned in the Río Grande.

John Doe: Left home, friends, and family in search of work and a better life. Died in the desert as an unidentified person, and now rests in a foreign and unmarked grave, as his family is left to wonder where he is.

Jane Doe: Left home, friends, and family in search of work and a better life. Died in the desert as an unidentified person, and now rests in a foreign and unmarked grave, as her family is left to wonder where she is.

Postscript

The Border Angels' work never ends as we continue to have *Marcha Migrantes* February 2 every year (in 2013, we moved our *Marcha Migrante VIII* up to join Javier Sicilia in the national "Caravana por la Paz"). We have also debuted several movie projects, including a movie with Sharon Stone entitled *Border Run*.

"When I was hungry, who gave me to eat?
When I was thirsty, who gave me to drink?"
Mathew 25:35

BORDER ANGELS
ANGELES DE LA FRONTERA

Sherman Heights Community Center Office
2258 Island Avenue
San Diego, CA 92102

P.O. Box 86598
San Diego, CA 92138

(619) 269-7865 ▪ enriquemorones@cox.net
www.borderangels.org

Another development, produced and written by good friend Josefina López, *Detained in the Desert,* was inspired by Border Angels, as was another, *Harvest Empire,* by Wendy Thompson. The *Love Has No Borders* concert series continues as well as presentations and debates at schools across country and service learning trips to San Diego.

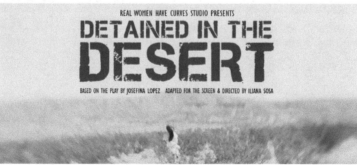

*For more complete information
about the Border Angels,
visit their website at http://www.borderangels.org/*

This volume experienced its final typeset on Wednesday, June 2, 2015, by the
working hand of Guillermo Nericcio García for San Diego State
University Press, using *Constantia*, a font developed by the
not-always-evil cyber geniuses that work for Bill Gates
at Microsoft. Nericcio García dedicates his
work here to the memory of our desert
sojourners who have fallen, and to
their shades that they may
find some final
paz.

Illustration, this page, by the late, great Rini Templeton.